YOUR
DOG
AND YOU

YOUR
DOG
AND YOU

A GUIDE TO A HEALTHY LIFE
WITH YOUR BEST FRIEND

JOE INGLIS

JOHN BLAKE

Published by John Blake Publishing Ltd,
3 Bramber Court, 2 Bramber Road,
London W14 9PB, England

www.johnblakepublishing.co.uk

First published in paperback in 2010

ISBN: 978 1 84454 953 5

British Library Cataloguing-in-Publication Data:

A catalogue record for this book is available from the British Library.

Design by www.envydesign.co.uk

Printed in Great Britain by CPI William Clowes, Beccles, NR34 7TL

1 3 5 7 9 10 8 6 4 2

In loving memory of EP

Contents

Introduction

In the many years I've been a vet – and lifetime of being a dog owner – I've experienced all aspects of the way we live our lives with our dogs. The one factor I've identified as being at the heart of our dogs' lives is the quality of the relationships between owner and dog. When these relationships are good, dogs and owners benefit from happier, healthier lives together. But, when they break down, all manner of health problems – from behavioural to physical – can develop.

In *Your Dog and You* I've used my veterinary training and personal knowledge of dogs, along with input from other passionate dog experts, to produce a guide to building and maintaining a healthy long-term relationship with your dog from puppyhood right up to old age. If you follow my philosophy, I truly believe that your dog's life – and your own – will benefit.

The basis of my philosophy of how we should live with our

dogs stems from the long and fascinating history that exists between our two species. Since they were first domesticated by our stone-age ancestors, dogs have been our constant companions. From feral hunters one step removed from wolves to cosseted lap dogs bred to resemble our human babies, *Canis lupus familiaris* has come a long way in the last 15,000 years.

The history of the domestic dog is a lesson in the power we hold over the animal kingdom. We have transformed the wild wolf into modern companion dogs, tailoring them to fulfil roles as diverse as family pets and invaluable assistance dogs, and, in doing so, changed a species almost beyond recognition.

My great-great-great-grandfather, Charles Darwin, saw the great evolutionary power of natural selection, and how it shapes every natural being from amoeba to humans. He also recognised the way in which artificial selection by man can change the natural world, and was fascinated by pigeon breeding, where he could see firsthand the effects that human selection could have on the very nature of a species. If Darwin were alive today, the incredible diversity of dogs that we have created from the simple wolf would, I'm sure, only serve to reinforce his views on the incredible power of selection.

With this power comes responsibility. By selectively breeding dogs over many thousands of years, we have created our domestic dogs as surely as if we'd had supernatural powers. Every feature of the modern dog from the shape of their faces to their character and personality has been created by our breeding decisions, so we have to accept responsibility for the health issues that arise from creating our companions in this way, and for the lives we ask them to lead with us in our modern worlds. How far we take that responsibility is a matter for personal debate, but there is no doubt that, if we choose to breed and own dogs, we have a moral obligation to look after their wellbeing.

Accepting responsibility for the wellbeing of our canine companions is one thing, but putting it into practice is another matter entirely. Just how do you square the needs of an animal (which, despite our best efforts, is still very much a wolf in a lap dog's clothing) with our hectic, twenty-first-century lives? And what level of basic needs should we provide? Some people lavish their dogs with lifestyles more suited to human beings, with state-of-the-art medical care and gourmet meals – but is this fair, does it make the dog happy, and, if not, what is appropriate and where do we draw the line between being a responsible pet owner and an indulgent one?

Answering these questions is part of what this book is about, but I'm also offering a solution – a philosophy for life with your dog. I passionately believe in the central importance of building a healthy relationship between you and your dog to the benefit of every aspect of their health and wellbeing – physical, emotional and mental. This book isn't an encyclopaedia of veterinary care or behavioural advice, but a guide to a healthy, happy lifestyle for animal and handler alike.

In the first chapter, I explore the most fundamental issue of all – choosing a dog. The cornerstone of a healthy relationship with a dog is finding the right animal to suit you and the life you lead. Get it wrong and, much like a bad marriage, there is little hope of long-term happiness. Get it right, however, and you and your dog can look forward to enjoying a wonderfully fulfilling and healthy lifelong relationship.

In Chapter Two, I look at puppyhood. The first few months of your dog's life are when the strongest bonds are made between you and your dog, and also where some of the biggest dangers lie. Shaping the mind and body of your puppy into a well-adjusted, happy adult is the best gift you will ever give to your dog, and in this chapter I will show you how it is done.

The formative months that make up canine adolescence are the subject of Chapter Three, where I examine the many dilemmas that this crucial period can present. As well as considering the impact of exercise and diet on your dog's physical health, I will also discuss the often contentious issue of neutering, before moving on to the theory and practice of training your dog.

How you live with your dog on a day-to-day basis is fundamental to building a successful relationship with your dog, and in Chapter Four I will explain how your routines and your everyday interactions with your dog, such as mealtimes, walks and simple family time, influence your relationship and happiness with your dog.

Chapter Five is all about food and here we'll take a detailed look at what to feed and what not to feed your dog, as well as tackling the always controversial topic of raw versus commercial diets. There's also a glossary of ingredients to help you fully understand what is in the food you feed to your dog, and a selection of my favourite home-cooked recipes for dogs.

The final three chapters in the book cover topics related to the breakdown in a relationship between owner and dog. Chapter Six looks at the psychological issues related to relationship breakdown and their manifestations as behavioural problems including inappropriate behaviours, fear and aggression. Chapter Seven moves on to consider two major physical health problems which are linked to the way in which we live our lives with our dogs, obesity and arthritis.

And finally, in Chapter Eight I consider the impact of old age on your dog and your relationship with a mature animal. I look at how lifestyle, exercise, diet and veterinary care all have a part to play in keeping your dog fit and active for as long as possible, before covering probably the most challenging subject of all – euthanasia. Knowing when to call it a day for your treasured friend is vital, and in many ways you can do more for your dog at this stage of their life than you can during their healthy years.

In writing this book I have used my 13 years of experience as a practising vet, as well as a lifetime of being a pet owner, to bring together a philosophy of dog care that I believe can transform the lives of pet dogs. I hope you will enjoy following my advice, and build a healthy, lifelong relationship with your dog. But, if you take just one message from this book, it would be that the key to understanding how to lead a happy life with your dog lies in your relationship with your dog. Build a healthy life together and you will both reap the benefits, not just in physical and mental health, but in all manner of ways which you may never have expected. A healthy relationship with your dog can release magic into both of your lives.

ONE

Choosing the Right Dog

If I was asked (and I often am), 'What is the single most important factor that contributes to a dog's health and wellbeing during its lifetime?' my answer would be: 'Choosing the right dog.' What I mean by this answer is not necessarily a black and white, objective choice of a 'good' dog or a 'bad' dog; it's more about choosing the right dog for you and your circumstances. There are some clear health implications of selecting certain breeds and types of dogs, but the suitability of the dog to your lifestyle is often of more importance than the simple pros and cons of any given breed.

For example, the Border Collie could be the most wonderful dog in the world if you are a Welsh hill farmer or agility enthusiast. If you're a little old lady living in a small flat in a city centre, however, the same dog would be likely to suffer from a range of behavioural and physical problems related to his unsuitability to the environment and lifestyle imposed on him.

Understanding the nature, both physical and mental, of different dogs is crucial if you are going to choose the right dog and build a happy and healthy relationship with your pet.

But, before we take a look at the dogs, even more fundamental to this process is taking a good look in the mirror and working out what kind of dog owner you are going to be. Your circumstances, lifestyle and opinions are all important factors which can be used to work out your 'canine category', which can then be used to help select the right type of dog for you. Get this right, and the chances of your having a long and healthy relationship with your dog are much higher than if you ignore these factors and just go for a dog because of emotional or other reasons such as initial cost or availability. Of course, emotion and personal preferences play a big part in selecting any pet, but, if you can sense-check your choice using the following method, both you and your dog stand to gain enormously.

So how do you work out which canine category you fit into? Well, it's really simple, and the first step is to answer the following five questions as honestly as possible:

1. Would you see your dog as 'one of the family'?
   a) Not at all – a dog is a dog and needs to know his place!
   b) To a point – the dog is part of the family, but definitely the least important member.
   c) Yes – a family is not complete without a four-legged member.
   d) Absolutely! My dog is the most important member of the family!

2. Is your dog a pet or a worker?

a) Worker – dogs enjoy work and my dog will earn his keep.

b) Both, but mainly a worker.

c) Mainly a pet.

d) A pet through and through! You wouldn't expect children to work, so why should my dog!

3. When would you take your dog to the vet?

a) Only in an emergency.

b) If required but not regularly.

c) Regularly, for routine vaccinations and treatment when required.

d) Whenever necessary, with no expense spared.

4. If your dog were very ill with a serious disease, what would you do?

a) Have him put to sleep as soon as he's in pain or not able to work.

b) Offer palliative treatment only to keep him comfortable.

c) Investigate the cause and consider reasonable medical or surgical treatments.

d) Pursue every treatment option regardless of cost.

5. Do you agree with pampering your dog?

a) No – dogs are animals not playthings.

b) Not really, but the occasional treat doesn't hurt.

c) Yes – but within limits (sunglasses and diamond collars are a step too far!).

d) Absolutely – a dog needs to be made to feel special, and whatever I can afford, he'll get.

Once you've answered these questions, add up your score by allocating one point for every 'a', 2 points for 'b's, 3 for 'c's and 4 for 'd's. Your total score will then give you your broad canine category:

5–10: Functional – you see your dog as a primarily working companion.

11–15: Caring – a dog is an everyday companion, but not a number-one priority.

16–20: Committed – a dog is a friend and companion to love and care for.

21– 25: Passionate – your dog is at the centre of your life.

When you have ascertained which basic category best describes you, we can then be a bit more specific and define more closely your exact canine category, which in turn will then give you some accurate pointers as to the qualities and attributes you should be looking for in your new canine companion.

Read through the descriptions of the three sub-categories under the broad category that the above questions have directed you to, and choose the canine category that you feel best describes your attitude and situation. You can then take a look at the list of key attributes and qualities associated with your category. These will be crucial to consider when we come to the next stage of the process of finding your ideal dog – looking at the dogs themselves.

FUNCTIONAL dog owners tend to fall into one of three categories – Country Lifers, Sporting Captains and Trophy Hunters.

Country Lifers

Your life is all about the country – walks, hunting, shooting, fishing – and a dog is a vital part of this lifestyle and integral to everything you do. However, your dog is no pampered pooch – he needs to earn his keep and not complain about sleeping out in a kennel or fetching pheasants from bramble thickets.

What to look for in your dog:

Physical – fit, strong and hardy.

Character – loyal, obedient, easily trainable, brave.

Sporting Captains

Whether it's flyball, agility, dog sledding or CaniX (running with your dog), sport and exercise are at the heart of your relationship with your dog, who is more a team member than a pampered pet.

What to look for in your dog:

Physical – matched to specific sporting requirements but likely to include stamina, fitness and agility.

Character – intelligent, receptive to training, enthusiastic.

Trophy Hunters

Winning in the show ring is what it's all about, and your dedication to the aesthetics of dog showing is your number-one passion.

What to look for in your dog:

Physical – a good, healthy example of your chosen breed.

Character – well mannered, patient, sociable.

CARING dog owners represent a large proportion of the 'everyday' dog owners and can be subdivided into the Child Appeasers, Dedicated Followers of Fashion and Accidental Heroes.

Child Appeasers

You're not 100 per cent convinced about owning a dog, but can see how happy it will make your children, so you're willing to bring a pet into the family to keep the peace!

What to look for in your dog:

Physical – small to medium size, healthy constitution.

Character – friendly, submissive, obedient.

Dedicated Followers of Fashion

To you, a dog is an accessory that says something about you and your values, whether it's a butch dog like a Staffordshire Bull Terrier (Staffie) that gives you respect on the streets or a top-price pedigree Poodle that wins you admiring glances in the park.

What to look for in your dog:

Dedicated Followers of Fashion tend to choose dogs that match their character, so, if you are loud and proud, consider a Standard Poodle or Labradoodle Cross; if you are more feminine, think about a Chihuahua, and if you're all man, the dog for you could be a Dobermann or Rottweiller.

Accidental Heroes

You never really wanted a dog but, for some reason, one has come into your life and you're both going to have to make the best of it. It could be the pampered lap dog of a recently deceased auntie or a stray that's come in off the road, but whatever the circumstances you're prepared to give the dog a home.

What to look for in your dog:

Accidental Heroes often have little choice and have to take the dog that fate delivers!

COMMITTED dog owners prioritise their dog as a central part of their lives, and include Family Men or Women, Newlyweds and One Man and His Dog types.

Family Man (or Woman)

A family can't be complete without a dog who will be a valued and well-loved member of the family team and be a companion for children and parents alike.

What to look for in your dog:

Physical – fit, healthy and robust.

Character – loyal, obedient, receptive to training.

Newlyweds

As a new couple, married or not, you see a dog as the first step towards building a family together.

What to look for in your dog:

Physical – easy to care for, small to medium size.

Character – loving, submissive, easy going.

One Man and His Dog

With no children or family, you see a dog as a close companion to share your life, joining you at work and play, and then curling up at your feet in the evening.

What to look for in your dog:

Physical – sturdy, appropriate size for your lifestyle.

Character – loyal, obedient, owner focussed.

PASSIONATE dog owners include the Pooch Pamperers, the Lonely Hearts and the Child Substitutes.

Pooch Pamperers

Your dog will be the centre of your life, with money and attention in ample supply. You believe that nothing is too good for your best friend. From home-cooked dinners to the best canine fashion, he will want for nothing!

What to look for in your dog:

Physical – small breeds.

Character – intelligent, full of character, loyal.

Lonely Hearts

With no one else on whom to lavish your love, your dog will become your best friend, confidant and companion, accompanying you everywhere and providing you with support and comfort.

What to look for in your dog:

Physical – generally not as important as character.

Character – loyal, obedient, owner focused.

Child Substitutes

As a couple without children, you look to your dogs to take on these roles in your lives, and you'll reward them with the love and care normally reserved for children.

What to look for in your dog:

Physical – usually larger breeds, but a wide variety of shapes and sizes can appeal.

Character – outgoing, energetic, full of life and enthusiasm.

Joe's Surgery Casebook

A NEW DOG FOR DIANE

Diane Wilson had recently lost her old Labrador, Barney, who'd been a loyal family pet for nearly 15 years, when she asked my advice about getting a new puppy. I was in the process of developing my 'canine category' idea, so I asked her to road test an early version – and the results were very interesting. I think we both expected her to fall into the 'family woman' category, as this would certainly have been the best fit for her as a dog owner with Barney, who was a valued and integral part of a family which included three children. However, after pondering my questions for a while, and reading about the various categories, Diane placed herself in the 'Pooch Pamperer' group, a surprise to us both.

'Barney was always the family's dog,' she explained, 'but

now, with the children older and my husband away a lot with work, I think it's time for me to have a dog for me. I'm not sure I'd have ever thought of myself as a "Pooch Pamperer", but I can see that that's the category that best describes how I feel about my next dog.'

With this new insight into the kind of dog owner she was going to be, Diane decided not to replace Barney with another Labrador, and instead found herself a delightful Bichon Frise bitch, who she's called Ella. `

'She's simply adorable – and she's fitted into my life so well,' Diane told me on a recent visit to the surgery with Ella for her inoculations. 'I'm so glad I took the time to really think through what I wanted in a dog, as it's made me – and Ella – so happy as a result.'

Celebrity Pets

HANDBAG POOCHES

We've all seen pictures of celebs like Paris Hilton carrying their Chihuahuas from photo shoot to A-list party in a designer handbag – and probably reacted with a shake of the head, convinced that this is surely the very worst example of dog ownership. But I think if you look at the lifestyle of these busy celebrities then their choice of pet doesn't seem quite so unsuitable. In many ways, one could argue that, although their approach to dog ownership may not suit you or I, it may be just as appropriate as a more traditional family pet suits a young couple with 2.4 children.

This might sound like a strange argument from a passionate dog lover, but I think that a successful owner–dog relationship is built on the compatibility between pet and owner, so consider whether there is a more suitable companion for a toy dog such as a Chihuahua, who doesn't really enjoy long walks or boisterous play, than an image-conscious celeb who's willing to pamper them? I may personally not be a big fan of the extreme inbreeding that has led to the exaggerated features of many modern toy dogs such as the Chihuahua, but if we accept that they are here to stay (at least for the time being) then we also have to accept that the unconventional lifestyle of the A-list may be most appropriate for these particular dogs, too – it's a strange world indeed!

You should now have a better understanding of how a dog is going to fit into your life, as well as the general characteristics that you need to look for if your new companion is going to live happily alongside you. Now it's time to turn our attention to the dogs themselves so you can really start to narrow down the field and find the perfect match for you.

Rather than go into detail on specific breeds, which is really beyond the scope of this book, I'm going to instead introduce ten major breed groups, along with a few example breeds from each. It's worth mentioning that there are many ways to classify breeds, and there are many different grouping systems used by different breed associations and organisations. I've grouped the breeds by their evolutionary origin which I think makes it far simpler to understand the general characteristics of the breeds in each category. I've also suggested which of my canine categories each group is most suited to – these are by no means exclusive suggestions, but will give you an idea of which breeds fit best with you and your lifestyle.

1. **Flock guardians** are one of the smaller breed groups in the domestic pet world – but, in terms of the history of our canine companions, they represent a far more significant group of breeds. Flock guardians, such as the Pyrenean Mountain Dog, were bred many centuries ago with the sole aim of creating dogs that could guard flocks of sheep, often high up in mountain pastures. This evolutionary history led to their primary characteristics – large dominating physical size, bravery, single-mindedness and territorial possessiveness – which are not always ideally suited to life as a modern pet dog. Many of these breeds tend to be slightly out of context as pets, often too big, too shaggy and too single-minded to make ideal companion dogs. But, having said that, there are many for whom a Spanish Mastiff or Pyrenean Mountain Dog makes the ideal companion.

Ideal for: Child Substitutes, One Man and His Dog.

2. One group of breeds that has made the best transition from their original roles as working dogs to household companion dogs is the **gundog**. This large group of breeds includes all of those dogs who were originally bred to help the hunter with a gun, and includes a wide variety of breeds from Water Retrievers such as Poodles to Field Spaniels and Pointers. Gundogs tend to be the most intelligent breed, having been selected for traits such as problem-solving ability as well as physical attributes such as swimming ability or agility. Many modern gundogs still work at their original roles, flushing prey from the hedgerows or chasing down a fallen duck and

bringing it back to the hunter's feet – but many more now spend their days retrieving nothing more than toys in the garden. Breeds such as the Golden Retriever, Poodle and Springer Spaniel are among the most popular companion dog breeds, with owners appreciating their usually placid nature, intelligence and physical enthusiasm.

Ideal for: Country Lifers, Sporting Captains, Child Appeasers, Family Men, Newlyweds, Child Substitutes.

3. Probably the most physically active and demanding dogs belong to the **herding dogs** group, which includes breeds such as the Border Collie, Australian Shepherd and German Shepherd. Bred originally to be working dogs trained to help farmers round up and manoeuvre stock in the fields, these dogs tend to be highly strung, with plenty of nervous energy and enthusiasm for exercise. Not breeds for the fainthearted, herding dogs nonetheless can make excellent companions for those owners with the time, energy and experience to build a strong relationship with them and take advantage of their exuberant natures.

Ideal for: Country Lifers, One Man and His Dog.

4. **Mastiffs** are a group that include such breeds as the Bull Mastiff, St Bernard, Doberman Pinscher and Bulldog. The majority of these breeds were developed with aggressive activities in mind, such as home or farm defence, or fighting, and this has led to lingering tendencies towards aggression in many Mastiffs. The reputation of breeds such as the Doberman may be

exaggerated, and the majority of individuals may be placid and well mannered, but there's no denying the fact that there is an inherent aggression within these breeds. For that reason they are usually best suited to owners with experience and the strength of character to enable them to dominate and control these dogs.

Ideal for: Dedicated Followers of Fashion.

5. Dog breeds have developed around the world, with those from the northern reaches of Europe, America and Asia generally grouped together as **Nordic Dogs**. These breeds, which include the Siberian Husky, Chow Chow, Finnish Spitz and Alaskan Malamute, have all developed from working dogs that lived with indigenous people in the snowy wastes of the northern latitudes. The majority was used for heavy work such as pulling sleds, and this physical strength and work ethic has remained in the modern versions of these breeds. Usually placid and well mannered, these dogs can make excellent companions provided that great attention is paid to their physical needs, including their absolute requirement for plenty of exercise.

Ideal for: Sporting Captains, Country Lifers, Dedicated
Followers of Fashion, One Man and His Dog.

6. The **pariahs** are a small group of breeds, with the Basenji probably the most common example. Pariahs in the more general canine sense include modern wild 'breeds' such as the Australian Dingo, and are considered to be most closely related to the wild canine ancestors that roamed the world many

millennia ago. It is hard to generalise about these breeds as there are so few to describe, but the Basenji, which descended from central African wild dogs in the 1800s, certainly makes a wonderful pet.

Ideal for: Trophy Hunters, Dedicated Followers of Fashion.

7. The **scent hounds** number among their ranks more breeds than any of the other groups, including the Beagle, Fox Hound, Deerhound, Wolfhound and Bloodhound to name but a few. These breeds generally date from the eighteenth and nineteenth centuries when fox and deer hunting became mainstream activities and dogs were bred to help every type of hunting activity. They tend to be headstrong and single-minded, with a tendency to follow their noses rather than the instructions of their owners, but they are still very popular as pets and can make excellent companions.

Ideal for: Country Lifers, Trophy Hunters, Dedicated Followers of Fashion.

8. The next breed group to consider are the **sight hounds**, which, as the name suggests, is a group originally bred to hunt by sight (as opposed to smell). The most typical example of the sight hound group is the Greyhound, which typifies the lightly boned, sleek appearance of these breeds. Sight hounds tend to be elegant dogs and have passionate devotees in the dog world, while leaving other dog owners cold to their physical appearance. They also tend to be slightly aloof and are

not ideal for those owners looking for a demonstratively affectionate dog. Despite this, they do make very loyal and trustworthy companions for those who fall for their charms. Common sight hound breeds include the Greyhound, Afghan Hound, Saluki and Borzois.

Ideal for: Family Men, Newlyweds, One Man and His Dog, Child Substitutes.

9. Of all breeds, the **terriers** retain a clear physical attribute that their original breeding created more clearly than most – their diminutive size. Terrier breeds were developed with the single purpose of hunting animals underground, such as rabbits and badgers. To this end, terriers were selectively bred for both their size and their tenacious natures, making them fearsome hunting machines that could tackle animals far bigger than themselves. Modern terriers often retain these personality traits as much as they do the physical attributes, making them feisty breeds – as all vets who've been bitten by an angry Jack Russell Terrier will attest to! Having said that, there are many terrier breeds who make really great family companions, including my personal favourites the Border Terrier and Norfolk Terrier.

Ideal for: Country Lifers, Family Men, One Man and His Dog, Lonely Hearts, Child Substitutes.

10. The final group of breeds is the **toy dogs**. These dogs, which often draw on mixed ancestry with links to many of the other groups, have one thing in common – they have been

bred specifically to be companions. Unlike most of the other breed groups which have generally become companion dogs after being bred for an original working purpose, most toy breeds were specifically bred for characteristics suitable for companionship. The classic example is the Cavalier King Charles Spaniel which had its origins as a gundog, but after a few generations of selection for endearing physical attributes, such as a large head, bulbous eyes and loving nature, the breed had become a companion rather than a worker. Today, toy breeds such as the Pug, Papillon and Chihuahua are among the most popular in the world as the role of dogs in our society shifts away from work to pleasure and companionship.

Ideal for: Trophy Hunters, Child Appeasers, Dedicated Followers of Fashion, Newlyweds, Pooch Pamperers, Lonely Hearts, Child Substitutes.

Hopefully this overview of the major breed groups will have helped you consider the most suitable breeds that will suit you and your lifestyle. The next stage is to move from theory to practice and actually locate your perfect canine partner. There are various routes to consider.

FRIENDS AND FAMILY

The simplest route to finding a new dog is through personal contacts or recommendations. For example, a friend's bitch is having a litter of puppies, or someone in the village needs to find a new home for their dog. This can work really well, as you'll often know a lot about the dog and his history, and you can get a very good impression of how well he would fit into your life before committing to taking him on. The downside of this route into dog ownership is that you might find yourself with a very unsuitable dog because either you're under pressure from a friend or relative to help out, or you let your heart rule your head when confronted with an adorable litter of next door's pups! My advice would be to try to remain as objective as possible and remember that you and the dog will have to spend the next ten to fifteen years together. If you are not suited, just like an ill-matched human marriage, the outcome is likely to be bad for everyone involved.

I have seen so many cases where people have taken on dogs they really shouldn't have simply because they were trying to help a friend or relative. Sometimes this can work out OK, but in many instances the end result is a mismatch between dog and owner leading to health issues for the dog, particularly behavioural problems, and frustrations, guilt and unhappiness for the owner. It's often clear to me (and them) that it would have been better all round if they'd never taken the dog on in the first place, even if that might have caused a short-term initial problem in finding the dog a home. There are, of course, exceptions, but in general it's not worth compromising when it comes to matching a dog to your needs, as you and your new dog can only be happy together if you are well matched.

BREEDERS

Most people, particularly those looking for a specific breed of dog, will look to a breeder. The advantages of this route are obvious — you can be very selective about the type of dog you get, even down to his colour and exact conformation (important if you're a 'Trophy Hunter' of course), and this can help ensure that your dog is as perfect a match for your requirements as possible. However, there are also potential disadvantages to buying from a breeder, and you do need to be aware of these before you rush out and spend a small fortune on a pedigree dog.

The main disadvantage is that, unless you know the breeder personally or are recommended one by a contact, it's unlikely that you will have much idea about the quality of the person you are getting your dog from. When I say 'quality of person' what I mean here is that there are all sorts of people out there breeding dogs, and they range from the excellent to the disreputable and even downright fraudulent, and it can be very hard to know what kind of breeder you are dealing with. Of course, you can just trust instinct and luck, and hopefully you'll be OK — but the consequences of being unlucky are potentially very serious for you and your new dog: you may well end up with an unhealthy, unhappy puppy who never really recovers from a miserable start to his life; you may be overcharged or sold a dog who's not what he seems; and you may well be inadvertently supporting cruel breeding practices and serious animal welfare problems.

So how do you spot a good breeder and avoid a rogue? You can start by looking in reputable places, and the Kennel Club is a good place to start. Although they are limited in their powers and cannot guarantee that any of the breeders who register with them are perfect, you are much more likely to find a good breeder if you go through the Kennel Club. In addition to their normal register of breeders, they also now run an accreditation scheme for breeders which aims to improve welfare standards by regulating factors such as number of litters permitted per bitch, the use of health screening tests (such as hip dysplasia, the deformation or misalignment of the hip joint that can cause limping, and eye abnormality screening) and the socialisation of puppies. In addition, accredited breeders are required to provide new owners with information on key subjects such as parasite control, feeding and vaccinations, and also to be available for 'post-sales support' once the puppies have gone to their new home. All of these features make the accredited breeders scheme very valuable. You can find out more at the Kennel Club website (www.thekennelclub.org.uk).

Breed clubs are also a good place to find reputable breeders and again the Kennel Club website is a good place to start looking for links to particular breed clubs.

Unfortunately, many prospective dog owners tend to use other means to find breeders, such as small ads in local papers and adverts on the internet. While it's perfectly possible to find good breeders this way, the odds are stacked against you and there is a much higher chance that you'll find yourself dealing with a less reputable breeder if you rely on this kind of search.

However you find your breeder, it's well worth applying the same five-point test before you commit to a purchase:

1. Does the breeder invite you to their home and give you full access to the breeding areas?
2. Do you get to meet the mother in situ with her puppies?
3. Are all the dogs visibly healthy and content?
4. Is all the paperwork present and consistent? For example, check vaccination cards to make sure injections weren't carried out somewhere else, which might suggest the puppies were bred elsewhere.
5. Are you offered the chance to talk to satisfied customers and see their dogs?

If you answer 'no' to any of these questions, alarm bells should start ringing and, unless further investigation convinces you that all is well, it would be best to look for a different breeder. If you're happy to answer 'yes' to these questions, then you can be relatively confident that you're dealing with a reputable breeder, which is a great start in your hunt for your perfect new puppy.

Joe's Surgery Casebook

A BAD START IN LIFE

When Joanne and Steve Jones lifted their new puppy Collie up on to the consulting-room table for the first time, my heart sank immediately. Instead of the usual bundle of energy you'd expect, this puppy was dull, lethargic and clearly unhealthy with a large pot belly, thinning fur and dull eyes. In fact, the only thing about him with any get up and go was the army of fleas bouncing around on his back. He'd clearly had a very poor start in life and, as I checked him over, I enquired about his origins.

'We found him through an advert in the paper,' explained Steve, who was now becoming a little concerned as he watched me listening to the puppy's chest and looking into his eyes.

'It was a very friendly chap from Wales, who told us he bred Collies on his farm.'

'Did you see the mother and pups when you visited the farm?' I asked.

'Oh no – he suggested meeting on the motorway as he lived so far away, so we picked him up there yesterday.'

My heart sank even further, as it was becoming clear that Joanne and Steve had been duped by a rogue breeder – a suspicion that was confirmed when I checked the vaccination certificate they'd been given. The address of the veterinary practice that had done the injections was in Birmingham – nowhere near the almost certainly fictional Welsh farm that they'd been told was his place of birth.

Apart from the fleas and heavy worm burden, their new puppy had ear mites, diarrhoea and an infected bite mark on his nose. Thankfully we were able to sort out all of these issues and, in the long run, the puppy turned out to be a lovely dog, although he always suffered with hip problems throughout his life, the result of mild hip dysplasia inherited from his parents.

Steve and Joanne were relatively lucky, but thousands of other new dog owners are not so fortunate, and the dogs they excitedly bring home end up suffering lifetimes of health problems as a result of a terrible start in life and the ruthless cruelty of the puppy farmers who breed them.

RESCUE CENTRES

I'm personally a great fan of rescue centres and believe that every potential dog owner owes it to the thousands of dogs languishing in these centres up and down the country to at least consider a rescue dog. Unless your requirements are very specific – Trophy Hunters in particular probably aren't going to find what they are looking for this way – you may well find a dog that fits your needs very closely if you take the time to visit a few centres. There are numerous advantages of finding a dog this way. Firstly there's the obvious contribution to the welfare of the dog you rescue and to reducing the massive stray and abandoned dog problem we have in this country. Secondly it's one of the few chances you'll have to really get to know a dog before you take him on. You can spend time with the dog at the centre, and some may even let you have a trial period with the dog before you commit fulltime. And, as well as these personal experiences, you'll also benefit from the experiences of the dog's previous owners and that of the centre staff who will be able to provide you with some invaluable information about the dog's temperament, character and health.

Obviously there are drawbacks to taking on a dog from a rescue centre – many of them are only in these centres because of behavioural or physical problems that have led to their being rejected by their original owners. Also, by taking on an adult dog, you have much less influence over the development of the dog's behaviour and character. You are more restricted in choice, as there are certain types of dogs that tend to predominate in rescue centres, particularly Staffies, German Shepherds and Lurchers. I'm not entirely sure why this is, but it does seem to be the case in the centres I've visited, and makes finding other types of dog a little harder.

Having said all that, with a little perseverance and patience, it is usually possible to find a dog that fits your requirements, and I would always encourage any prospective dog owner to start their search at their local rescue centre.

Joe's Pets

JACK

When I decided the time was right to start looking for a new dog, the first place I went to was my local rescue centre – and it was one of the best decisions I've ever made. Against all the odds I found Jack on my very first visit and it really was almost a case of 'love at first sight'! Among the pens full of Staffies and Lurchers, there was a small black and white dog barking his head off as he bounced up and down in an attempt to catch my attention.

I liked the look of him straight away, and asked the kennel staff if I could take him out of the pen and see what he was like in person. As soon as he was out of the pen he calmed down and came straight up to me to say 'hello', and within five minutes I was sure he was the one for me. He matched my requirements almost to the tee – a lively, energetic dog who'd fit into a house with children and enjoy life in the country. As a Spaniel cross Collie he was physically everything I wanted in a dog, and his happy-go-lucky character and obvious good manners made him the dog for me.

It took a little while to complete the formalities, but by the end of the week Jack was settling in at home, and, in the three years since, we've never looked back and he's become a wonderful part of the family.

It doesn't always work out as easily as this, and sometimes first impressions can lie – but my experience does go to show how easy and successful rehoming a dog can be, if you're lucky!

THE FINAL DECISION – WHICH PUPPY FROM A LITTER?

If you've followed the thought process through this chapter you should now be in a position to be getting down to the very final stages of choosing your new companion. You may even be faced with a litter of equally adorable faces staring up at you and be wondering how on Earth you are going to choose between them. Well, apart from good old-fashioned intuition, there is a more scientific approach to take, and that's based on a series of tests to try to determine the puppy's character. Once you understand the individual characteristics of each puppy, you can use that information to help you select the right puppy for you to take home.

THE CAMPBELL TESTS

The Campbell tests are a well-established set of simple tests that can help quantify the nature of a puppy at around 6–8 weeks of age, and give you a limited, but useful insight into their basic character. There are five tests, and they are best performed in a quiet area away from the rest of the litter and other distractions. The tests need to be carried out by someone new to the puppy (so you as a prospective purchaser would be fine, but not the breeder).

TEST 1: ATTRACTION

Place the puppy on the ground in front of you and step back a couple of paces. Then clap your hands softly and observe the puppy's reaction:

1. He immediately runs to you, tail held high, and jumps up to lick you.
2. He immediately runs to you, tail held high, and scratches at your hands with his paws.
3. He immediately runs to you wagging his tail.
4. He comes to you hesitantly, tail and head down.
5. He does not come.

TEST 2: SUBMISSION

With the puppy sitting in the 'sphinx' position, stroke his back, applying gentle pressure to his head and back, and observe his reaction.

1. He struggles, scratches and finally turns over and growls and bites.
2. He struggles and turns over to scratch you.
3. He struggles at first before calming down and licking your hands.
4. He turns over on to his back and licks your hands.
5. He moves away from you.

TEST 3: FOLLOWING

Without calling the puppy, stand up and walk away from him, staying in view at all times.

1. He follows immediately with his tail held high, biting at your feet.
2. He follows immediately with tail raised but doesn't bite your feet.
3. He follows immediately but with his tail down.
4. He is hesitant but does follow you, with his tail down.
5. He doesn't follow you and moves away in another direction.

TEST 4: DOMINANCE

Stand the puppy up on his hind legs by holding him around the chest with both hands. Maintain this position for around 20 seconds.

1. He struggles forcefully, growls and bites.
2. He struggles forcefully but doesn't growl or bite.
3. After an initial struggle, he calms down and licks your hand.
4. He doesn't struggle, and licks your hand.
5. He doesn't struggle.

TEST 5: CONSTRAINT

Lay the puppy on his back and hold him in this position for 30 seconds with a hand on his chest.

1. He struggles forcefully and bites.
2. He struggles until he is free.

3. After an initial struggle he calms down.

4. No struggle and he licks your hand.

5. No struggle.

Once you have completed all five tests, take a look at the results and use the following guide to categorise the basic character of the puppy:

Majority of answers are 1: This puppy is likely to be dominant and aggressive and would not be suitable as a pet. The only time to consider a puppy in this category would be for a guard dog or working dog such as a police dog where controlled aggression is a desirable trait. Even in these cases, take care and make sure you are prepared to cope with a potentially dangerous dog, especially if it is a large breed and commit the time required for training.

Majority of answers are 2: A puppy with dominant tendencies that will require strict training and control. Most suitable for functional dog owners who put form and/or function ahead of personality and temperament.

Majority of answers are 3: These puppies are most likely to be well balanced and stable and have potential to fit into most roles, with the possible exception of Pooch Pamperers who may find them not quite submissive enough to fulfil their role as Child Substitutes or Pampered Pooches.

Majority of answers are 4: Submissive puppies which are likely to be less suited to working roles or stressful situations such as showing, but could fit into family roles well.

Majority of answers are 5: Puppies with scores at this

end of the spectrum are likely to be inhibited and to have been poorly socialised. They can be unpredictable and prone to fear-aggression behaviours (aggressive behaviour as a response to frightening situations) and so should be considered for all roles with some degree of caution.

With the information gleaned from the Campbell tests, you should now be ready to take the plunge and pick the puppy for you. While there are no absolute guarantees that your new companion will turn out to be the perfect dog, if you've been through the process described in this chapter, you will have given you and your puppy the very best chance of being a perfect match.

TWO

Puppyhood

The first three months your puppy spends with you are the most important of their life. During these crucial months your puppy's character will develop, their temperament will be defined and, most importantly, their relationship with you and the rest of the family will be formed. Mistakes during this time will have long-lasting effects and are often the primary cause of serious lifelong health problems, particularly behavioural issues.

So how do you get this period right? Well, there are several key elements to helping your puppy develop successfully into a happy and healthy adult dog, and, if you follow the simple guidelines I outline below, you'll be giving your puppy the best chance of growing up to be a dog to be proud of.

The most important factor to remember is that a puppy is not a human baby and, even though modern dogs are completely domesticated and comfortable with growing up in a human-dominated environment, they are still animals at heart and the transition from their mother's care to the confusing and often scary human world needs to be handled with care and attention. You need to remember that your puppy is moving from their 'natural' canine world to what is still, even after thousands of years, an artificial environment where strange animals that stand on two legs make the rules!

The number-one priority for helping your puppy make this transition is good old simple tender loving care. Puppies, like children, are highly impressionable and their characters are greatly influenced by the attitude and behaviour of those caring for them. Looking after a new puppy who is likely to be scared, vulnerable and intimidated by their new world with love, patience and attention is vital if they are to grow up trusting their human companions.

TLC is not to be confused with pampering or indulgence – over-doing the loving care can have an equally negative effect as under-doing it – but is simply a philosophy of looking after and caring for a puppy with empathy for their feelings and needs.

Joe's Surgery Casebook

A TALE OF TWO SPANIELS...
I often see several members of the same litter in the surgery once they've gone off to their new homes, and it can be fascinating to see how differently two siblings can turn out with two different families.

Recently I saw a litter of Springer Spaniel puppies in the surgery, and then, a few weeks later, had two of the male pups back in for their vaccinations. First in was Toby, who'd been chosen by a well-to-do family with a passion for shooting. Toby was destined for a busy life chasing down fallen pheasants in the Cotswold countryside, and was obviously eager to please his new master, with an enthusiastic tail wag and loyal brown eyes. The second pup had been named Defor (D for Dog!) by the children of the Jones family, and had a very different life ahead of him as a family pet. He too was full of the joys of spring on his first visit and he was obviously the pride and joy of the whole family.

By the time both pups came back for their second vaccinations, Defor was still the playful pup he'd been a couple of weeks previously, full of enthusiasm and happiness, but Toby was a completely different dog. He cowered when his owner picked him up, and looked suspiciously about him as he lay quietly on the consulting-room table. After his injection, a puddle of urine leaked out from underneath his tummy and he looked up at his master apologetically. His owner, far from reassuring the obviously scared pup, picked him up roughly and scolded him for his accident – an action which served only to further intimidate and alienate Toby and compound his misery.

A couple of years on and I still see both dogs regularly in the surgery. The difference between them is astounding; Defor is a happy, confident family dog who trots enthusiastically into the surgery, whereas Toby slinks in with his tail between his legs and invariably wees himself in the corner of the consulting room. There are obviously innate character differences between the two dogs, but a large part of the differences between them can surely be attributed to the attitude of their owners in those crucial early months.

It's hard to give a fail-safe guide for how to do TLC as it's a very personal thing and everyone expresses themselves in different ways. Moreover, the type of dog and their role in your life will also dictate to some degree how you interact with and care for your puppy. But, having said that, don't assume that, just because you've identified yourself as a Country Lifer, or a Sporting Captain, you don't need to show TLC to your puppy. A pup that's destined to work for his living or be paraded in the show ring needs to grow up in just as loving an environment as a dog with a lifetime of one-to-one pampering ahead of him – it's just that the form of that TLC might differ.

The real key to TLC is providing time and attention, with the details of how you interact being less crucial than your attitude and commitment to spending time with your new companion. Remember that, unless you are taking on more than one puppy, you will have to take on the role of entertainer and teacher in chief, becoming a substitute for your puppy's parents and siblings all rolled into one. Play is a crucial part of the developmental process, helping to hone a puppy's physical and mental skills, as well as creating emotional bonds between you, and should be something you prioritise during the first few months together. In fact, it is something you should never stop doing, as most dogs never really outgrow puppyhood at heart, and play remains a central part of the behavioural activity of adult dogs.

Beyond the personal preferences for TLC there are some absolute physical necessities that all dogs require if they are to settle into a home in a suitably caring environment:

A comfy bed

This doesn't have to be a designer faux-leather four-poster, but needs to be appropriate for the size of your dog (and remember your puppy will grow!), comfortable, easy to clean and situated in a warm and sheltered position, whether it be in the kitchen for a family dog or in an outdoor kennel for an outdoor dog.

Food and water

We'll come on to diet and feeding shortly, but a readily available supply of fresh water in a suitable bowl, alongside a feeding dish, is obviously essential for your new pup.

Toys

In the wild, puppies would hone their dexterity and agility by playing with their litter mates and with objects such as stones, twigs and leaves, so in the human environment we have to provide suitable substitutes. As previously mentioned, unless you have several puppies, you will take on the role of sibling as well as teacher, so provide a selection of suitable toys to take the place of everyday outdoor objects. There are countless thousands of puppy toys available and you need to choose ones which are both generally safe and also suitable for your individual dog. There's no point getting a large rope toy for a Chihuahua or a delicate squeaky mouse for a German Shepherd, for example!

One final point on TLC is to mention the concept of 'teaching love'. This might sound a bit new age, but, whether or not you agree with the use of the word 'love' in regard to a dog's emotions, there is a recognised technique for building a positive association between you and your puppy – and the end result is often a bond that can only really be described as a form of love, albeit an artificially manufactured form.

The technique for teaching love is very simple and is an example of one known as 'classical conditioning' which we will discuss in more detail later on. The idea is to build a subconscious association in your puppy's mind between you, your voice and smell with positive feelings such as those linked to rewards. To achieve this, you simply need to spend time with your puppy talking and interacting with him at the same time as giving him treats or kibbles from his dinner. Gradually, he will begin to associate you with the positive feelings he gets from the rewards, and after a while those feelings will persist even without the physical rewards being present, and, every time he sees or smells or hears you, he will feel that same positive emotion – which may or may not be true 'love' but has the same end result.

Ground rules and consistency are my next set of priorities when it comes to raising a happy, well-adjusted puppy. Without a clear and consistent set of rules to live by, puppies, like children, will become confused about their position and confusion invariably leads to behavioural problems and unhappiness all round. So it's really important to establish a set of ground rules from day one, and stick to them as consistently as you can.

Ground rules will obviously vary greatly from household to

household and from dog to dog, but there are some key ones that I think every dog owner should consider implementing:

'No go' areas

Establishing areas of the house where your dog is not allowed is not just a useful device for keeping parts of the house free from dog hair, it more importantly sets out clear physical boundaries. By having areas of the house that people are allowed into but the dog is not is a simple way of starting to teach your dog about the social order in the house and the difference between dog and human. You can choose whichever rooms or areas you like – but be consistent and stick to your decisions, otherwise you will immediately begin to undermine your authority and your dog will realise that your word is not binding – which has obvious implications for training and discipline.

Mealtimes

Feeding your dog after the rest of the family is often quoted as the correct approach as it maintains the disciplined order of the 'family pack', and setting out basic feeding-time rules is a good idea and helps get your puppy into good feeding habits for the rest of their life. My approach is to feed puppies at specific mealtimes and not in between, since in my experience the 'continual grazing' approach tends to encourage pickiness and fussiness as well as making it much harder to use food as part of a training regime. I'll go into the details of how often to feed later on in this chapter, but for now just remember that mealtimes should be regular and have a fixed duration.

Bedtime

There are many varying approaches to the issue of bedtime and sleeping arrangements. Some people maintain that leaving a puppy unattended overnight is bordering on cruelty, but the majority of experienced dog experts, myself included, argue that giving in to demands for attention at night and not leaving a puppy alone simply reinforces any fears they may have about being alone and makes everyone's lives, including that of the dog, miserable. In my experience, the approach that best balances TLC and discipline is to make sure your puppy has everything they need, including a comfortable bed, water and toys, settle them down for the night and then leave them until a time of your deciding in the morning. For the first night or two – but it usually is only one – they will cry for periods during the night, but any distress they feel will soon be forgotten and they will quickly become accustomed to sleeping on their own and be happy and more confident dogs as a result.

Before your new puppy comes home, have a think about ground rules and which ones are going to suit your family and your personal approach to bringing up your puppy. And then make sure you stick to them, through thick and thin!

Joe's Surgery Casebook

BREAKING THE RULES – PIPPA'S STORY

Pippa is a lovely dog – in small doses. She's a Jack Russell cross Collie and is full of happiness and energy, barking madly when you come to the door and jumping up relentlessly until you give her the attention she demands. This kind of energy and attitude is fun for a while, but after spending more time in her company you really start to feel for her owners, a middle-aged couple called Joan and Allen who bought Pippa a couple of years ago when their children left home.

'We wanted a friendly dog to keep us company,' explained Joan to me when I visited them at home recently to examine Pippa, who'd been off colour for a few days. 'But she's turned out to be such a handful, we're not sure we can cope with her any more.'

Thankfully there was little wrong physically with Pippa on this occasion, but it was clear that her behaviour was a big issue – and, if it didn't improve, Joan and Allen were seriously considering finding her a new home. Sadly this kind of outcome is all too common, and I could just see Pippa becoming more and more out of control and badly behaved if she ended up in the relatively chaotic environment of a rescue centre.

I spent a while talking to Joan and Allen about Pippa's behaviour and her upbringing, and it soon became clear that a lack of ground rules was at least partially to blame for her behavioural problems. Joan admitted that as a pup Pippa had been allowed to rule the roost, sleeping in their bed, getting them up at first light, and running wild throughout the house. I explained how this lack of early discipline was likely to have been an important factor in her subsequent development and current behavioural issues.

After my visit, Joan and Allen took Pippa to see a local dog behaviourist, and, when I saw her again a few months later, the change in her behaviour – and the attitude of Joan and Allen – was dramatic.

'She's a different dog,' explained Joan happily, giving Pippa a stroke, 'not perfect, but so much better than she was.'

Just goes to show you can teach an older dog new tricks – but also how much easier it is to teach young dogs properly from the start!

Last, and by no means least, of my key priorities for bringing up a healthy and well-adjusted puppy is socialisation. This refers to the process of introducing new dogs to everything they are likely to encounter later in life, so they are confident and, in the case of interactions with other dogs, have the social skills necessary for adult life.

The process of socialisation is really very simple – at its most basic, it is really just the process of introducing your dog to individuals and situations that they need to become accustomed to in a safe, unthreatening and calm environment. The theory goes that this then helps the puppy to be able to cope better in similar circumstances as an adult, which has great benefits in terms of their behaviour and social skills.

A good example is car travel. If the first time your dog experiences the bizarre (to a dog's mind) feeling of watching the world go by from the back of a tin box that makes funny noises and lurches back and forward and whizzes around corners is as an adult, it's not surprising to expect that they will be more than a little upset by it, and react with fear and confusion. If, on the other hand, they are introduced to the wonders of car travel from a very young age in a gradual and controlled manner, it is very likely that they will quickly learn to take the experience in their stride and become confident and happy passengers for the rest of their lives.

One of the key elements to socialisation is timing – there is a golden period between the ages of 8 weeks and 12 weeks when a puppy's brain is most open to learning and assimilating new ideas, and you need to take advantage of this period if you are to successfully acclimatise your puppy to the world in which they are going to live. This is one of the main reasons why early vaccination programmes are such a good idea, as they allow puppies to safely explore the world at a younger age. Back when I first qualified as a vet (in the mid-90s), the earliest age that puppies could be fully vaccinated was 12 weeks – right at the end of the socialisation window – and this placed significant restrictions on socialisation, as without the protection of a completed set of vaccinations it is unwise for a puppy to fully interact with other dogs and the world at large. Now, with vaccination programmes licensed to be completed by 10 weeks of age, those all-important final two weeks of the golden period for socialisation can be used to the full, helping significantly to improve the long-term behavioural health of puppies.

So, with the benefits and timeframe of socialisation established, what exactly should you be doing to socialise your puppy? Read most books on puppy training and there will be a list of activities, events and people that all dogs should be introduced to in order for them to be fully socialised, including the obvious ones such as car travel, other dogs, children and cats, and some less obvious ones including people in wheelchairs, skateboarders, postmen and vets. While these lists are useful, I think it is more productive to think about your personal circumstances and lifestyle, and draw up a list relevant to you and your dog's future, rather than simply trying to tick every box in a long generic list.

For example, if you are bringing up a puppy destined for the show ring, your top priorities would need to be that your puppy is impeccably socialised with other dogs, car travel and people, so they behave well and enjoy the lifestyle of attending shows that you have planned for them. Less crucial for your dog, although still important as secondary goals, would be socialisation with children, postmen and cats. If, on the other hand, your dog is going to be a family pet, socialisation with children is by far and away the most important goal to achieve, along with cats if you have a multi-pet household, and car journeys.

Celebrity Pets

MATT BAKER AND MEG

Of all the well-known pets I've met and in some cases worked with, former *Blue Peter* presenter Matt Baker's Collie Meg is certainly one of the best behaved, largely because Matt knew and understood the importance of socialisation – and applied it specifically to the rather unusual lifestyle that he knew Meg would lead.

From earliest puppyhood, Meg was destined to share the

limelight with Matt on *Blue Peter*, and this meant that she had to be absolutely comfortable with the potentially intimidating environment of the TV studio, where strange people, cameras and lights present a very stimulating and unusual environment – especially for a dog bred to roam the moors and round up sheep! Matt did exactly the right thing by brining Meg to the studio almost from day one, and giving her lots of fuss and attention, so the experiences of being in that environment were imprinted on her mind in a positive manner. These early days at Television Centre were crucial to Meg's development and she grew up to be impeccably behaved on set and took to her career as a TV presenter's dog with aplomb.

Had Matt been less proactive in his approach, or left Meg at home until she was older, perhaps under the illusion that it would be better not to expose her to such a stressful environment at such a young age, I'm sure that she wouldn't have turned out so well, and her life with Matt would have been poorer as a result.

DIET

You are what you eat is an old adage, and it applies just as much to our pets as it does to ourselves. Every day in the surgery I see animals with problems related to their diet, from simple upset stomachs to more serious, long-term issues such as food intolerances and growth problems caused by inappropriate diets, so it's clear to me how important food is for the health of our four-legged friends. And the most critical time of all is puppyhood, when getting the diet right will set your dog out on the path to long-term health. Getting it wrong can have negative impacts lasting for the rest of the dog's life.

Before I look at the details of what makes a good diet for a puppy, it's worth spending a little while considering the physiology of a puppy and their nutritional requirements, and how this impacts on what we need to feed them.

A puppy is, to all intents and purposes, a growth machine, dedicated to building a full-sized dog at the end of the 6–18-month growing period. In order to do this, it needs an ample supply of all the basic building blocks that dogs are made of, plus plenty of energy to put it all together. The most important building block is protein, as this is what makes up a large proportion of all animal bodies, from the tiniest antibodies in the bloodstream to the masses of muscle that make up the bulk of a puppy's body. Protein itself is made up of a series of molecules called amino acids, and the way in which these smaller building blocks are arranged dictates the structure and function of a fully formed protein. There are 22 recognised amino acids used by animals in the construction of proteins, and of these 10 are known as 'essential amino acids' which means they cannot be synthesised by the dog's body from other amino acids and must be supplied by the diet. For example, arginine is an essential amino acid that is vital for the immune system, liver function and growth rate among many other functions and it cannot be made by the dog's body so must be supplied by the diet. Without sufficient arginine in the diet, a puppy is likely to suffer from serious health problems including stunted growth and a weakened immune system.

Protein can come from many sources, including vegetable matter such as soya, but the best source of protein for puppies is, of course, meat. The reason for this is simple – when building an animal, it's easiest to use protein from another animal as this requires far less work compared to trying to build a dog out of vegetables! It is true that vegetable protein can contain all the amino acids a puppy requires, but the issue is that they will not be in the same ratios as the puppy requires, making it much harder work for the puppy's body. These proteins also produce more waste products as a result of being less well matched to requirements, and this has led to them being termed 'lower-quality' proteins than animal protein.

We can take this discussion of 'good' versus 'bad' proteins further by recognising that not all animal proteins are equally good or bad and there are certain types of animal protein that are better for dogs and particularly for puppies. Generally speaking, the white-meat proteins, such as poultry and fish, are considered to be a closer match to the requirements of canine animals than red-meat proteins such as beef, and therefore can be considered to be a better protein source. If you look at the amino acid profile of various meat proteins, it's only chicken and turkey which tick the box for every one of the ten essential amino acids that dogs require, whereas other meats, such as beef and most fish, only provide 70–80 per cent of these essential amino acids. Obviously, combining protein sources generally solves the issue of these missing amino acids, but it is still preferable to be feeding as a primary protein source one that provides as many of these essential amino acids as possible.

The final point to make about protein is that, as well as the variety of protein, there is also great variation in the digestibility of proteins, which can make as big a difference to the quality of a puppy's food as the inherent quality of the protein. For example, some vegetable proteins such as grains and vegetable extracts do provide a reasonable mix of amino acids, but, because they are very poorly digestible, it takes the body longer and more energy to extract the amino acids and make them available to aid growth.

Aside from proteins, the other essential nutrients your puppy needs as he is growing are fats, vitamins, minerals and energy. Fat may be a dirty word in human nutrition, but fats are essential for all animals with many vital roles in the body including the transport of fat-soluble vitamins and the provision of essential fatty acids. Puppies fed on ultra-low-fat diets have been shown to develop a range of health problems including poor skin, vision and mental abilities, so it's clear that all puppies require a certain level of fat for good health and development.

But are all fats good fats? The simple answer is no, but it's not as clear cut as with proteins. There are certain essential fatty acids that are considered to be particularly beneficial, such as omega 3 and omega 6 fatty acids, and there are some types of fat, such as saturated fats, that are generally considered to be 'bad', but in general dogs, like people, require a balanced mix of the good and the bad. A diet with no saturated fat would be as unhealthy as a diet with no omega 3 oils, so it's not just a question of selecting the good and removing the bad – a healthy diet has a mix of both.

Vitamins are a very loosely associated group of chemicals that are essential for many aspects of all animals' health. The definition of a vitamin is very loose – an organic compound that is required as a nutrient in tiny amounts and cannot be synthesised by the animal so must be provided in the diet. The range of chemicals that make up the list of 13 main vitamins is very varied, as are their functions. However, there are several that are of particular relevance to puppies, including vitamin A, which is crucial for the development of sight, and vitamin D, which plays an important role in the control of calcium levels in the body and thus the correct development of bones in the growing puppy. All commercial puppy foods will contain added vitamins which should ensure that minimum safe levels are met (and maximum safe levels not exceeded), so, as long as you are feeding one of these diets, you shouldn't need to worry too much about vitamins. However, they are more of an issue if you are feeding a home-prepared diet, of which more shortly.

Minerals are the inorganic equivalent of vitamins – compounds required in relatively small amounts that are not made by the body – and include staple molecules such as calcium, sodium, phosphate, copper and magnesium, all of which have vital roles within the growing body. Again, the correct levels of these molecules are generally assured in commercial foods according to agreed guidelines, but there is a very real risk of deficiencies or excesses if you are trying to feed a homemade diet to your puppy.

And last, but by no means least, comes energy, without

which your puppy would grind to a halt! Energy can come from all of the major nutrient groups – fat, protein and carbohydrate – so there is no absolute requirement for puppies to have any particular nutrient simply to provide energy. In general, most commercial puppy foods use carbohydrates from grains such as rice or wheat to provide the majority of the energy requirement. The fact that dogs don't absolutely require carbohydrate is an argument sometimes used to promote carbohydrate-free foods for dogs under the premise that in the wild dogs would gain very little, if any, energy from carbohydrate and therefore it's not 'natural' for domestic dogs to be fed carbohydrate. There are many flaws in this argument, not least that just because animals didn't eat something in the wild doesn't mean they can't benefit from it as domestic animals. Most animal nutritionists would agree carbohydrate is a healthy and easily digestible energy source and plays an important part in the provision of affordable, convenient pet foods.

With the theory behind us, it's time to take a look at what it means in practice when it comes to choosing the right diet to feed your puppy at home. There is a bewildering array of ready-prepared commercial foods available for puppies, as well as books and internet sites offering recipes for home-cooked diets and even raw feeding regimes. So how do you pick between these diets and choose the one that's best for your puppy? As with choosing a puppy in the first place, it largely comes down to you and your circumstances: the right diet for one person and puppy may not suit the lifestyle or needs of another owner and pet. I'll go through the different types of diet available, and their advantages and disadvantages, before showing you how you can choose the right diet for your pup.

COMMERCIAL DIETS

The term 'commercial diets' is used to describe the vast range of pre-prepared foods available for dogs of all ages, and they broadly fall into two categories – wet and dry foods. Wet foods, which include tinned and pouched foods, are, as the name suggests, made with a high proportion of water, usually up to around 80 per cent. Dry foods, on the other hand, are generally hard, dry biscuits containing very little moisture – typically around 7 or 8 per cent. Both types of food can provide perfectly healthy nutrition for your puppy, but there are various pros and cons with each:

Wet food
Pros: Usually very palatable
High water content maintains hydration
Cons: Less convenient to use and serve
Tends to be worse for dental health

Dry food
Pros: Very convenient to serve
Better for dental health
Cons: Can be less palatable than wet foods
Some concerns over effect on hydration

I'll discuss the details of how wet and dry foods are made, and how this affects their quality, in a later chapter, but for now it's enough to say that both wet and dry foods can provide the nutrition your puppy needs, and that, in most cases, offering both gives your puppy the best of both worlds.

As for selecting the specific type and brand of food, whether it be wet or dry, I would urge you to remember one key piece of advice – read the label, and read it thoroughly. All commercial puppy foods will contain all the nutrients a puppy needs for its basic health, but there is much more to healthy nutrition than simply meeting minimum levels. As we've seen, there is a great difference between proteins in terms of their digestibility, and between different fats in terms of their quality, so bear this in mind when selecting food. And then there's the crucial issue of what's *not* in the food, which in many ways is just as important as what is in it.

Unfortunately, the vast majority of commercial pet foods contain a range of artificial chemical additives including flavours, preservatives and colours, and these ingredients can have a major impact on the health of your puppy. Many of these additives are banned from the human food chain due to concerns over their safety, such as colours like tartrazine and preservatives like Butylated hydroxyanisole (BHA), yet they are permitted under pet-food regulations which simply classify them as 'Permitted Additives'. I will go into this area in more detail later, but for now the key message is to read the label, understand as well as you can what is in and what is not in the food, and make an informed choice.

**CHOOSING A COMMERCIAL PUPPY FOOD –
WHAT TO LOOK FOR:**
- Quality meat such as chicken, lamb or fish as the primary protein source
- Moderate protein level – between 24 and 30 per cent in dried foods
- High fat/oil level – between 15 and 18 per cent in dried foods
- Omega 3 fatty acids

And what to avoid:
- Poor-quality proteins such as soya, 'meat and animal derivatives' and vegetable extract proteins
- Artificial additives including colours, preservatives and flavours

One final piece of advice on this subject is to try to be as objective as you can in making your choice and resist the temptation to believe the marketing messages that are thrust at you by manufacturers. Just because a product has the word 'natural' or 'nature's' in the title, or there's a picture of a juicy breast of chicken on the front of the pack, it doesn't necessarily mean that the food inside is either natural or made from fresh chicken breast. Always remember that the pet-food companies are trying to persuade you to buy their foods, and some will use some fairly inventive and sophisticated techniques to help convince the unwary pet owner!

HOME-COOKED DIETS

I've been an advocate of home cooking for pets for many years and believe that properly prepared meals can be an excellent supplement to the everyday diet consumed by both dog and puppy. However, I would not recommend feeding a home-cooked diet exclusively to any dog, and puppies in particular, unless you are experienced and knowledgeable about the subject. It is all too easy to feed an inappropriate diet and cause health problems if the puppy is relying on your home-prepared meals as their only source of nutrition. For example, calcium is an essential mineral that puppies require for healthy growth of their bones, and sadly many simple home-cooked recipes are surprisingly low in this crucial nutrient. Chicken and rice, a staple home-cooking recipe, contains far too little calcium (and several other nutrients) for a growing puppy, and, if you were to feed just chicken mince and rice to your puppy, there is a high chance that you could cause serious health problems including skeletal deformities. And fresh liver, a classic ingredient in many home-cooked dishes, can also cause problems if fed too regularly, not through a deficiency but an excess of vitamin A, which can also lead to bone problems.

So, unless you have particular knowledge of canine nutrition and can plan and prepare a diet that delivers all the essential nutrients and avoids the potential dangers, I would recommend home-cooked meals only as an adjunct to a commercial diet.

Joe's Cookbook

HOME-COOKED TREATS FOR YOUR PUPPY TO ENJOY!
Meaty Rice Pudding
Something of a treat, this recipe is packed full of wholesome nutrients – carbohydrate from the rice, protein from the meat and calcium from the milk. This recipe makes enough for several meals, keep it in the fridge for a few days – or better still, invite a few friends with puppies around and have a puppy party!

To make enough for a puppy party, you will require:
- 125g rice
- 750ml milk
- 150g beef or lamb mince
- 1 teaspoon Marmite

Method
Preheat the oven to 180°C, 350°F, Gas mark 4.

Mix all the ingredients together in a large oven-proof dish. Place in the oven and cook for about 75 minutes, stirring frequently for the first 45 minutes and then leave to cook, uncovered, for the final 30 minutes. Leave to cool for at least an hour before serving.

Puppy Cheesy Treats
These tasty biscuits are an ideal treat or snack for a hungry puppy. Use them to help with training by rewarding good behaviour – but make sure you don't overdo them as they are quite rich and fatty. One or two treats a day as part of your training schedule is ideal.

For enough treats to last a couple of weeks, you need:
  50g wholewheat flour
  150g grated cheddar cheese
  50g butter
  1 clove garlic, crushed
  1 beef stock cube, crumbled
  50–100ml milk

Method
Preheat the oven to 180°C, 350°F, Gas Mark 4.

Put the flour and butter in a large bowl and rub together until they form a crumbly mixture. Add the grated cheese, crushed garlic and crumbled stock cube and mix well. Slowly add milk to the mixture until it forms a very sticky dough. Flour your hands and start kneading the dough until it forms a single firm lump. Then turn it out on to a floured surface and roll it out to about ½ inch thick.

Cut the dough into puppy-sized biscuits using a small pastry cutter – or, if you don't have one, try using the end of an apple corer – this cuts out the dough into just the right sized little rounds.

Place the biscuits on to a greased baking tray and cook in a moderate oven for 15–20 minutes, until they are golden brown. Allow to cool before giving to your puppy. Stored in an air-tight container, these will keep for one or two weeks.

Liver and Banana Milk Shake
This might sound pretty unpleasant to you, but puppies will go

mad for this healthy shake! It's full of the goodness of liver and the natural nutrients you can only get from fruit such as banana. Either serve on its own or pour over dry dog food – either way he'll lap it up.

For enough for two or three puppy drinks, you'll need:
   Small piece of liver (about 100g)
   1 banana, peeled and chopped into four pieces
   $^{1}/_{2}$ pint milk

Method
Place the liver in a large bowl and cover it with boiling water. Leave it to cook for ten minutes and then drop into a blender. Add the banana and milk. Blend everything together and serve straight away.

This will keep for two to three days in the fridge.

RAW FEEDING

I'll cover the often contentious subject of raw feeding thoroughly in a later chapter, but it's worth giving a quick overview here with specific relevance to feeding puppies this kind of regime.

Raw feeding has grown in popularity over the last few years, championed by books such as *Give Your Dog a Bone* by Ian Billinghurst, and it is now the feeding regime of choice for many dog owners worldwide. Advocates of raw feeding claim it is far healthier than feeding commercial diets as it is 'closer to nature' – a fact which its opponents question, who also express serious concerns about the safety of this kind of diet where dogs are eating foods including raw poultry.

The approach recommended by Ian Billinghurst is summarised by a paragraph from his book which explains his key recommendations for feeding a puppy:

The bulk of a puppy's food should be raw meaty bones
The rest of the puppy's food should also be raw
Puppies should always be kept hungry and never grown
at their maximum growth rate
Puppies should learn to eat everything

While I would agree to some limited extent with points three and four, I cannot agree that a diet consisting of raw bones and raw meat is the best way we can feed our puppies in the twenty-first century, and I personally believe that well- formulated, natural commercial foods represent a much better combination of healthy nutrition, safety and convenience.

There is not the place to analyse these arguments in detail, and it's a subject I will return to in a later chapter, but I would simply recommend extreme caution before considering a raw diet for your puppy. I'm sure in the right hands a raw diet can work well, but there are so many potential dangers and pitfalls for the less experienced pet owner that it is a very risky route to take. I also don't personally believe that the benefits of raw feeding are significant, which makes the balance of risk versus reward even less appealing to me, particularly in the case of puppies whose diet and health risks are so important to consider.

SELECTING THE RIGHT DIET FOR YOU AND YOUR PUPPY

As you can see, there are many factors to consider when deciding what kind of diet to feed your puppy, not to mention the bewildering array of brands you'll be confronted with if you opt for commercial food. However, there are some simple questions to consider that should help make this decision a little easier:

Q. Is your dog a large or small breed?

A. If your dog is very small, the chances are he will be happier on a predominantly wet diet, including some home-cooked food. Small and toy breeds can eat hard dried foods, but the majority of these dogs do prefer the easy-to-chew wet foods, and fussy individuals often respond well to tasty home-cooked meals fed in addition to commercial wet foods.

Larger breeds tend to enjoy both wet and dry food, but dry food often works out to be more economical and easier to feed due to the quantity of wet food that large dogs require – a cup full of dry biscuits is easier and usually cheaper than several tins or trays of wet food.

Q. Are you worried about mess and smell?

A. If you're not keen on messy and smelly dog foods in

the house, then dry foods are the answer. Wet foods tend to be stronger smelling and messier, particularly when storing half-eaten sachets or tins of food or when it comes to the build-up of residues in your puppy's food bowl.

Home-cooked and raw feeding regimes are definitely not ideal for clean and tidy pet owners and are only really suitable for those of us who don't mind getting our hands – and kitchen – dirty!

Q. Do you have the time to devote to home-prepared meals?

A. Preparing meals for your dog at home can be time consuming – and surprisingly expensive – so only consider using home-cooked or raw diets if you're prepared to put in the time, and money.

The conclusion for most new puppy owners is that commercial foods are the best option, and feeding a mix of both wet and dry foods is ideal

HOW OFTEN TO FEED?

This is a key question and it's important to get the frequency and timing of your puppy's meals right as this is crucial for not only their physical wellbeing, but also their training and behaviour.

Most puppies will be weaned by six weeks and settled on a solid diet by the time they head off to their new home at around eight weeks of age. Many breeders will send their puppies away with detailed instructions on diet, with recommendations on types of food, timing and special requirements for their particular breed, such as tea and Weetabix in the morning, or an omelette for lunch (seriously!). While it's important to consider these recommendations and certainly gradually make changes to a settled regime, it's also worth remembering that most breeders are not necessarily experts on nutrition and often have other factors in play influencing their views, such as supplies of particular brands at discount prices. So pay attention to what you are told if your puppy does come from a breeder – but don't be afraid to change things if you are not happy with the regime they have recommended.

In general, puppies of eight weeks of age should be being fed four meals a day, dropping down to three by twelve weeks of age, and two by sixteen weeks. These meals should be evenly spaced through the day, and each mealtime should be a distinct event, with a set time and duration. Puppies that get used to grazing on their food for long periods of time will be much harder to train later in life as they become used to food being available on demand and therefore less motivated by food as a reward for training or good behaviour, so it's important that your puppy gets used to eating their food in a single sitting.

My preferred method is to offer the puppy a dish of food and leave it down for 10–15 minutes, giving them ample time to eat until they are full. At the end of this time, if there is any food left over, take it away and don't feed again until the next mealtime.

The timing of meals is as important as their duration, and, whenever human and canine mealtimes are close to each other, the single most crucial thing to remember early on is to get your puppy used to eating after the rest of the family have had their food. This is one of the fundamental building blocks of the 'family as pack' theory of behaviour and instils in your puppy a sense of place in the family that leads to an inherent respect for the 'more important' pack members – you and your family. So make sure you sit down to your breakfast, lunch and dinner before feeding the puppy their meals – otherwise the newest member of the family pack might get ideas above their station about their status, and this can be the precursor to all manner of behavioural problems later in life.

Joe's Pets

PAN AND BADGER

My first experience as a puppy owner took place in 1997 during my first year as a qualified vet. My then wife-to-be, Emma, and I brought home two tiny Border Collie puppies from a farm in the North Devon hills, and named them Pan (after a favourite childhood book of mine) and Badger (because of his black and white striped head). Although qualified vets, we were both relatively inexperienced puppy owners and made many of the typical mistakes, including feeding a low-quality commercial puppy food that gave them both terrible diarrhoea. Changing to a better-quality food took more of our limited budget (newly qualified vets are not as well paid as you might think!) but immediately paid dividends as the diarrhoea stopped and both dogs were quickly and visibly stronger and brighter.

After some arguments as to the best way to feed the puppies, and which ground rules to enforce, we quickly began to understand the importance of regular mealtimes and controlled feeding. This approach paid dividends in the long term, as both dogs grew up to be motivated by food and therefore easy to train, and well-behaved and well-socialised dogs who know their place in the family pack.

HOW MUCH TO FEED?

This is one of the trickiest questions when it comes to feeding puppies. The obvious answer would be to follow the instructions on the packet of commercial food, but these tend to be far too generalised to be of any significant use, and in many cases can be more of a hindrance than a help. Lots of puppy owners bring their underweight or overweight puppies in for vaccinations and are amazed when I tell them that they are over- or under-feeding. 'But I'm feeding exactly what it says on the tin!' they exclaim, before I explain that, rather than looking at the tin, they should be looking at their puppy as the best guide to the correct amount to feed.

This is the key point to remember – all dogs are individuals and the only reliable way to know if you are feeding the correct amount is to take a look at your puppy and assess their condition. If they are too fat, it's obvious you are over-feeding; if they are too thin, then they could do with an increase in their daily rations – easy! Feeding guidelines on commercial foods are fine as a starting point, but don't rely on them blindly while your puppy is obviously losing weight or piling on the pounds.

Assessing a puppy's condition takes some practice and expertise, but the general principle holds true – looking at your puppy is far more valuable than looking at the packet when it comes to assessing your puppy's feeding regime.

To help with this process, I've devised a very simple condition-scoring system to help you assess whether or not your puppy is on the right track (I'll introduce a more detailed version later on when we discuss obesity). All you need to do is run your hands along their flanks and assess whether or not you can easily feel their ribs. If the ribs are very prominent – it feels like running your fingers down a piano keyboard – then your puppy is likely to be underweight and you should increase their rations; if you can barely feel the ribs at all under loose skin and fat, then your puppy is overweight and you should consider feeding smaller portions; and if your puppy lies somewhere between these two extremes, then the chances are your current regime is about spot on.

So, in conclusion, if you're feeding a commercial food, use the feeding guidelines as an initial guide to how much to feed every day, but thereafter try to rely more on your own evaluation of your puppy's condition. If in doubt, consult your vet or vet nurse who will be able to help you accurately assess your puppy's weight and feeding requirements.

PREVENTATIVE HEALTHCARE – VACCINATIONS AND PARASITE CONTROL

We've discussed choosing a puppy, looked at training and feeding, and now it's time to consider the role of the vet in your puppy's life and how they can help you protect your puppy against diseases and parasites.

Firstly and most importantly are vaccinations. These injections, which are generally given between the ages of six and ten weeks, are the cornerstone of protecting your puppy and keeping them healthy, and have been immensely successful in all but eradicating diseases such as distemper, and massively reducing the incidence of other potentially fatal diseases such as parvovirus and leptospirosis over the last 30 years or so.

In the UK, we protect puppies against five main diseases – distemper, parvovirus, para-influenza virus, infectious hepatitis and leptospirosis – and there are also additional vaccinations for rabies and kennel cough. Each of these diseases is potentially life threatening, and modern vaccines offer the safe and reliable protection which is essential for all puppies. There are always scare stories about the risks of vaccinations but the reality is that, while there are risks of side effects with any vaccination (as there are with any medical treatment, for that matter), the benefits far outweigh the risks. In my experience as a vet, I've seen many cases of serious diseases such as parvovirus killing unvaccinated puppies, but I have never seen or heard of a fatal reaction to a vaccination, so I would wholeheartedly recommend vaccinations to all puppy owners.

The specific vaccination regime recommended by vets does vary depending on the brand of vaccine and occasionally on local requirements, but in general dogs can usually have their first injection at 6–8 weeks, followed by a second at 10–12 weeks. Full immunity is not conferred until around a week after the second injection, so it's advisable not to take your puppy out and about in public places until this time. However, as we've previously discussed, it is important to start the socialisation process as early as possible, and it is OK to take your puppy to meet other dogs which you know are fully vaccinated in a safe environment (such as a home or garden) once your puppy has had their first injection. Most puppy training classes will also accept puppies once they've had their first injection, and it's worth considering starting at this young age as training a young dog is much easier than trying to teach an older dog new tricks!

In some areas and for some breeds, your vet might recommend additional vaccinations, particularly against parvovirus which is still prevalent in many inner-city areas. Some breeds including Rottweilers appear to be particularly vulnerable to parvovirus and many vets will offer an additional third injection against this disease at 16 weeks of age.

After the initial course of vaccinations, adult dogs require booster injections on an annual basis to keep their protection up to date. In the past we used to give all five vaccinations annually, but recent research has shown that only the lepto-spirosis and para-influenza vaccinations need to be given every year, with the others administered every third year. This regime reduces the number of injections your dog has to have and should go some way to assuaging the fears of those people who believe that too many vaccinations are linked to diseases (although, as previously mentioned, there is little evidence that this is true).

Did you know?

Distemper in dogs is caused by a virus that is so similar to the human measles virus that many years ago dogs were protected against distemper by using the human measles vaccine! And that's not all, it has also been claimed that children living in households with dogs who have been protected against distemper using a live vaccine will be protected against catching measles – although this is not something I would recommend testing in practice!

While we're on the subject of vaccinations, a quick word of warning about some of the so-called alternatives out there. In recent years the growing popularity of alternative remedies has led to an increase in the use of homeopathic 'nosodes' in place of traditional vaccinations. There are many alarmist websites which make unsubstantiated claims about the danger of vaccines, and promote these nosodes as a safe and effective alternative. This is a very dangerous practice as there is absolutely no evidence that nosodes produce any protective effect whatsoever, and, by encouraging people to avoid vaccinations, the promoters of these alternatives are endangering the health of not just the individual animals that are not vaccinated, but whole populations, as vaccinations are only truly effective at wiping out diseases if sufficient numbers of animals are protected. As seen by the rise in cases of measles in children in recent years as a result of the MMR scare discouraging parents from vaccinating their children, it only takes a small drop in the number of vaccinations to allow a disease to take advantage of the chinks in the protection and cause infections.

Advocates of homeopathic nosodes make very confused claims about how they work and why they are safe. Apparently, they are similar to traditional vaccines, stimulating the immune system to react against the virus that causes the disease, but manage to do this without any risks of side effects because they are so diluted as to contain no actual particles of the disease at all! It really is very bad science, and apologies if you are a fan of homeopathy, but there is no place for nosodes in the prevention of serious disease, either in animals or people, so please steer well clear and trust the science behind real vaccinations to protect your puppy!

Did you know?

VACCINATIONS – WHAT'S REALLY IN THEM AND WHY DO THEY WORK?
Modern vaccination programmes are based on the well-established theory that, by introducing a small amount of a safe version of a disease agent (virus or bacteria) to the body's immune system, the body will react by producing antibodies.

These antibodies will then protect the body against infection by the real infectious agent if and when the animal comes into contact with it later in life.

The safe versions of the disease agent can either be killed viruses or bacteria, or what's called an attenuated version, which means that the virus or bacteria has been altered to make it non-pathogenic (not disease causing). Live attenuated vaccines are generally more effective and give longer-lasting protection, which is why we only need to give injections against diseases such as parvovirus (which use a live vaccine) every three years, compared to annually for leptospirosis and kennel cough, for which there are only killed vaccines available.

Another component of many vaccines is an adjuvant, often made from parts of an unrelated bacterium, or even a mineral such as aluminium, which boosts the effectiveness of the vaccine. The exact details of how this effect works is not always clear, and there have been scare stories related to potential adverse effects of adjuvants in some vaccines, particularly in cats, but in general they are accepted as a safe and beneficial additive to most vaccine preparations.

The second key preventative medication that your puppy requires is worming treatments. Intestinal parasitic worms are incredibly common in dogs, but particularly so in puppies who are usually infected by their mothers via the milk. Heavy worm infestations can occasionally lead to health problems including weight loss, diarrhoea and general poor condition, but, more often than not, worms don't cause any major health problems. So why worry about them? It is important to make sure your puppy doesn't have a heavy worm burden as this can cause them health problems, but probably the most important reason to treat regularly for worms is for human public health. The canine roundworm *toxocara canis*, the most common intestinal parasite of puppies, can cause major health problems for children if they ingest the larvae of the worm, which are found in the faeces of infected animals. The problem occurs when the larvae of the worm find themselves in the wrong kind of animal and can't complete their usual lifecycle. This can lead to the larvae developing abnormally and in abnormal parts of the body, including, in very rare circumstances, the eye, causing blindness in the child.

So it is definitely advisable to worm your puppy regularly, if only to reduce the risk to children from the worm larvae. Most vets would advise regular treatments every 2–4 weeks between birth and four months of age. The simplest way to worm puppies is with worming tablets which kill off any adult worms in the intestine. Vets supply the most effective tablets, so it is worth getting your wormers from your vet, as many pet-shop treatments are ineffective.

As with vaccination, there are alternative worming treatments available, including homeopathic preparations and herbal preparations. While it's tempting to dismiss the likely effectiveness of homeopathic alternatives, I do believe that certain herbal preparations have the potential to be effective in controlling worms. Many traditional medications are based on herbal extracts, so it is not surprising that combinations of herbs can be effective in some circumstances. Having said that, I would still urge caution and only use herbal preparations to treat worms if you are confident about the efficacy and safety of the mixture as some will be worse than useless, and might even cause harm. For example, wormwood is often used as a 'natural' worming treatment, but if used regularly this herb can lead to serious liver and kidney damage. Many other herbal wormers include laxatives, which can have deleterious effects on the bowel as well as being of questionable effectiveness.

I would recommend traditional worming treatments from your vet, administered every 2–4 weeks until four months, and then monthly until six months of age. There are no recognised risks associated with the majority of these treatments, and there is a definite public health benefit to regular treatment, alongside benefits to your puppy's own health.

Last, and by no means least, on the preventative treatments front, fleas are one of the most common external parasites of young dogs, so protecting your puppy against them is very important. Heavy flea burdens can cause many problems, including skin conditions and even anaemia as fleas are blood-sucking parasites which live on the blood of host animals. Fleas can also transmit diseases and other parasites, including a canine tapeworm which is passed on to dogs when they eat fleas from their backs.

There are many ways to protect against fleas, but the most common treatments nowadays are spot-on preparations that you simply place on the back of the dog's neck. The active ingredients then spread through the fat layer of the skin, without entering the bloodstream, and kill off any fleas that land on the animal. These treatments are generally very safe and effective and can be used on puppies from as young as eight weeks of age (although always check the particular product you are using to make sure). Most require monthly or bi-monthly application and many also protect against other parasites including ticks and mange mites.

Joe's Surgery Casebook

ALTERNATIVE TREATMENTS – A CAUTIONARY TALE

Eileen's reputation as a passionate advocate of alternative treatments was well known at the practice – she was convinced that conventional treatments were inherently unsafe and that homeopathy and herbal remedies were much better alternatives. In fact, it was a surprise that we ever saw her at all given her views, but she did occasionally relent and begrudgingly accept that antibiotics were useful in the most extreme cases, so we saw her and her unruly pack of German Shepherd dogs a few times a year.

Then one day she rushed into the surgery with a young puppy in her arms who was obviously in a very bad state. I took them through to the consulting room and could immediately see that the puppy was dangerously ill – bright-red bloody diarrhoea stained his back end, and his skin and eyes showed the telltale signs of severe dehydration. The diagnosis was straightforward: the puppy had parvovirus.

Sadly, the puppy was too ill to be saved and died at the surgery early the following morning. It was a particularly tragic case because parvovirus is entirely preventable and, had Eileen not been so convinced of the evils of vaccinations and the protection that her homeopathic remedies would guarantee, this puppy would not have suffered and died.

After this sad case, Eileen was forced to reconsider her views and now has all her puppies vaccinated – but only against parvovirus. She still maintains her general anti-vaccination view, which I find very strange given what happened. At least she's seen sense and given her dogs the protection they deserve against one disease.

A final subject to touch on before we leave puppyhood and start thinking about the period of adolescence is toilet training. This is often an issue that causes concern for dog owners, with many differing schools of advice each claiming to offer the best and most reliable technique. However, personally I think toilet training is one of the easiest aspects to bringing up a dog as it simply involves honing your puppy's natural instincts. Dogs, like most animals, are instinctively clean. In evolutionary terms, keeping toilet functions separate from living and eating areas has benefits for the health of the pack. So teaching your puppy to go to the toilet outside involves nothing more than demonstrating the difference between the living areas of his world – indoors – and the outdoor environment where it is acceptable to go to the toilet.

The basic tool for getting this message across is, as with all training, positive reinforcement – praise and attention when he goes in the right place rather than punishment when he doesn't. Stick to this idea, banish thoughts of newspaper on the kitchen floor, and you'll soon have a perfectly well-toilet-trained puppy!

THREE

Adolescence

As your puppy grows up, they will pass from puppyhood to a period of adolescence when they become sexually mature and grow to their full adult size. This period, usually between four and twelve months of age but sometimes much longer, is just as crucial as puppyhood in terms of the potential for good and bad effects on your dog's future health and wellbeing. Therefore, it's important to understand the changes your dog will be going through and how you can help your puppy grow into a healthy adult.

Dogs are quick developers. Unlike humans who take decades to mature into adults, most dogs are fully grown and capable of reproducing by the time they are a year old. The reason for this speedy development is obvious – in the wild, there is precious little time to spare in the literally dog-eat-dog world where immature animals are vulnerable to predation, disease and all the other risks the wild world poses. Out on the plains of Africa and in the woods of Europe where the wild dog and wolf evolved many millennia ago, there was selection pressure on these canine ancestors to make sure puppies matured into adults as quickly as possible so they could fend for themselves and survive to pass on their genes.

Obviously there are not the same pressures on modern dogs – and in fact there are some very different selection pressures, of which more will be said shortly – but the effects of this historical evolution are very much built into modern dogs which have retained their quick-paced development despite their much changed environment.

In the last few thousand years, other selection pressures have also left their mark on the development of our puppies into adult dogs. Artificial selection by humans for specific traits such as size has had a significant impact on the way in which certain types of dog develop – and this is very important to understand when considering the growth of our modern puppies. For example, selection by ancient Irish hunters for large dogs which could protect people from wolves and other predators led to the development of the modern Wolfhound, the largest breed of dog in the world. However, one side effect of selecting for such a large dog is that it takes far longer for these animals to reach their full adult size – usually at least 18 months compared to as little as six months for some toy breeds of dog – and this has a great impact on how these dogs should be looked after in this extended adolescent period.

The main effect that adult size has on the adolescent growth period is the requirement of the dog for certain levels of nutrients, particularly protein (the basic building block of growth) and minerals such as calcium and phosphorus. In small-breed dogs that reach their full adult size by eight or nine months of age, the requirement for these nutrients is higher (as a percentage of the food they eat) than for much larger breeds which grow at a more sedate pace. It is very important to get these levels right, as feeding too light a diet to a small animal could lead to nutritional deficiencies, and, more dangerously, feeding a rich diet to a large-breed dog can contribute to growth spurts that lead to potentially serious complications including joint damage.

The risks of excessive growth in large-breed dogs are very real, and I see many dogs in the surgery that end up with lifelong joint problems which are directly related to excessive growth rates in their adolescence. These joint problems, which are usually termed OCD (osteochondritis dissecans), are caused by poor cartilage formation in the joint, and can lead to serious long-term complications with arthritis. In addition to OCD, rapidly growing large-breed dogs can also suffer from other bone disorders including panoestitis, which is a term given to inflamed long bones and causes shifting lameness, and various forms of joint malformation, including hip dysplasia and elbow dysplasia.

The link between diet, growth rate and these diseases has not been conclusively proven, but there is sufficient evidence to make it highly likely that there is a link, in addition to other factors such as genetics and exercise (of which more shortly). Therefore, it is sensible to ensure that you feed your growing adolescent dog appropriately for his breed and size and minimise the potential for growth spurts and subsequent joint or bone problems. The best and safest way to achieve this is to use a commercial diet specifically formulated for your puppy's size – there are many brands available that produce foods designed for young growing dogs of small, medium or large breed; these will be designed to deliver the optimum mix of nutrients to give your puppy the best chance of growing up healthily.

In addition to selecting the correct diet for your adolescent dog, understanding how exercise affects the growing canine body and tailoring an exercise regime to suit their growing bodies is just as crucial. And, as with diet, it is the larger-breed dogs that are most at risk of health problems related to exercise during adolescence.

The problem with exercise in young growing dogs again comes back to their ancestry. Back in the ancient wild environment, dogs were all roughly the same size – wolves are similar in stature to most medium-sized modern dogs – and there were no giant or very small dogs in existence. These mid-sized dogs evolved their skeletons to cope with the rigours of exercise during adolescence, as it was obviously crucial that wild dogs of all ages could run to hunt and escape attack whatever their age.

However, after many thousands of years of human artificial selection, many modern dogs are so far removed from the original 'design' that the delicate balance between the structure of the skeleton and the size of the dog has been lost.

Many dogs are now either much smaller or much bigger than they evolved to be, and this leaves them vulnerable to problems when faced with the stresses and strains of exercise at a young age. Large-breed dogs are particularly vulnerable as their skeletal systems can be under immense pressure as they try to grow into the giant dogs we've artificially created. Their bones and joints are under far more stress than those of smaller dogs, and take much longer to reach their adult strength. It's therefore not surprising that things can go wrong when these dogs are pushed to their limits before they reach full maturity.

Over-exercising large dogs at a young age can contribute to very similar problems as over-feeding and growth spurts – OCD lesions in the joints, elbow and hip dysplasia – as well as additional conditions including cruciate ligament rupture in the stifle (knee) joints and stress fractures.

It's obviously important to avoid over-doing it with large-breed adolescent dogs, but what exactly do we mean by 'over-exercise' and how do you balance the quality of life implications of not exercising a dog with the health risks of physical activity? Unfortunately, there are no easy answers and it's a question at the heart of my philosophy of living with your dog which requires each dog owner to evaluate their own views on risk and welfare.

If you ask a veterinary orthopaedic surgeon, whose job it is to treat the worst cases of OCD and hip dysplasia, they will tell you that large-breed dogs should never be exercised off the lead until they are at least 18 months of age. But how realistic is that recommendation for the average dog owner who wants to enjoy their life with their dog – and how fair is it on a dog whose life expectancy might only be seven or eight years (which is not uncommon in the largest breeds of dog)?

My view, as a vet and dog owner, is that you need to adopt a balanced approach and try to steer a course between the two extremes of total protection but poor quality of life on the one hand and increased risk of long-term joint damage but better short-term quality of life on the other. I believe that it's not realistic or fair on a dog to restrict them to lead-only walks for the entirety of their adolescence – imagine if you were told you could never run as a child and think about how frustrating that would be. Nevertheless, it is clearly irresponsible as the guardian of your dog's long-term health to put them at risk by ignoring the evidence linking excessive exercise to joint disease. So you need to think about your personal feelings on this issue and make a decision based on your own philosophy – but always remember to have your dog's welfare at the front of your mind. It might be that you could not bear the thought of restricting your dog's freedom, in which case you'd err towards the risks of more exercise, or it could be that you're more concerned about the long-term prospects of your dog so you decide to take a more cautionary approach. Whichever route you choose, just be aware of the risks and implications for your dog's wellbeing and keep that at the forefront of your mind.

Joe's TV Casebook

NEWFOUNDLANDS TO THE RESCUE

In my role as the resident vet on *The One Show* on BBC 1, I met many dogs of all shapes and sizes, but one particular dog on the show demonstrated one solution to the exercise conundrum facing the owners of large-breed dogs.

The dog in question was a Newfoundland. These enormous dogs definitely fall into the category of dogs at risk of joint problems related to their size and amount of exercise during their adolescent period. Yet the owner of this dog, who also had several other 'Newfies', told me that he'd never once had any joint problems with any of his dogs despite their exercising rigorously from a young age.

When I watched the film of his dogs for the show, before talking to him live on the set, it was quickly clear what his secret was: swimming. These dogs were no ordinary dogs, they were surf rescue dogs trained specifically to pull drowning swimmers from the sea. Swimming is one of the few forms of exercise that has little impact on the joints and is far safer for growing dogs than running on solid ground.

Newfies are particularly adapted to swimming, but there's no reason why any dog can't exercise in water, and it's well worth considering as one way of allowing your growing dog to exercise without risking their long-term health. There are more and more hydrotherapy pools available nowadays which offer a safe swimming environment for dogs if you're not lucky enough to live by the sea or near a safe river, so you should be able to find a suitable swimming site wherever you live.

NEUTERING

The next big topic we need to consider during the period of adolescence is a contentious one for many dog owners. The idea of emasculating a male dog or removing the womb and ovaries from a bitch doesn't sit easily with some people for a wide variety of reasons ranging from worries about the effects of the operation on a dog's character or appearance, to issues of status, particularly with male dogs, and even anthropomorphisms, leading to worries about the dog's welfare based on how the owner would feel in their dog's place.

Before we address these arguments, it's worth being absolutely clear about what the castration and spaying operations do and how they affect the animal, as there is often a surprising amount of confusion on both points. Firstly castration; this relatively quick and simple operation involves the removal of both testicles from a male dog, thus rendering the dog completely infertile and removing the main source of the male hormone testosterone, which affects temperament, character and physical attributes. The operation is always performed under a general anaesthetic and is usually carried out through a small incision just in front of the scrotum. Recovery is quick, with most dogs being back to their old self within a few days, and the incidence of complications is very low.

The only occasional complicating factor arises when one or both testicles have failed to descend, a condition referred to as cryptorchidism. In these cases the un-descended testicle needs to be located and removed, as, if it is left in situ inside the body, there is a high risk that it will turn cancerous due to the higher temperature of the body compared to the scrotum where the testicles are designed to live. Finding and removing the un-descended testicle is not always straightforward and can involve a major abdominal operation if the testicle is retained deep within the abdominal cavity. Recovery from this kind of operation is usually longer and more difficult than for a straightforward castration.

For female dogs the neutering operation is always a major undertaking and carries with it more significant risks than the male equivalent. The operation, which is usually referred to as spaying (as opposed to 'spading' which is often what clients at the surgery call it!), involves removing the entire womb and both ovaries via an abdominal incision. The fact that the operation involves entering the abdomen, and removing the ovaries which have a large blood supply directly from the aorta (the main blood vessel from the heart to the body), makes it far trickier to carry out than castration and there is always the potential for complications including life-threatening internal bleeding – although I must emphasise that this is very rare.

Being able to successfully carry out a spaying operation is one of the defining parts of learning to become a competent small-animal vet, and it often takes months, if not years, of practice before most vets feel completely happy undertaking this operation. In fact, many vets, myself included, feel that the spaying surgery is one of the most challenging operations vets are faced with, so it's not surprising that it takes a while to really get the hang of it.

There are different approaches to the operation but in general an incision is made in the midline, just behind the umbilicus (belly button equivalent). When your dog goes home, she will have a series of skin stitches in a wound that is usually between 3 and 10cm long (depending on the skill of the surgeon – more experienced surgeons tend to operate through a smaller incision which makes for a less painful and quicker recovery). Beneath this skin incision will be another series of sutures in the muscle wall of the abdomen, and it is these sutures that are really critical in the recovery process. If the dog over-does things too soon after the operation, these internal sutures can rupture, which can lead to one of the most common complications of the surgery – a wound breakdown and hernia of abdominal contents under the skin. If this happens, you'll notice a swelling in the site of the operation and probably some pain and discomfort, and you should get her back to the vet quickly to have the breakdown repaired.

Wound breakdowns are unpleasant and delay healing, but they are not usually life-threatening, unlike the most serious complication of spaying surgery which is internal bleeding. This situation is a nightmare for all vets, and usually happens because the ligature placed on the blood vessel leading to one of the ovaries works loose and allows bleeding from this high-pressure artery. This usually happens during surgery, in which case the surgeon can locate the problem and tie another ligature to stop the bleeding, but occasionally it can happen later on. This is when things can get very dangerous, as the dog is no longer under anaesthetic and a second operation is required to stop the bleeding. Thankfully, this is incredibly rare, and personally, in 13 years of veterinary work, it has only happened to me once – but, as you'll see from my case-book report below, once is more than enough for any vet to deal with.

Hopefully, this detailed description of all the things that can go wrong with spaying surgery hasn't scared you – it's important to be aware of how major the operation is, as well as the potential risks but, in practice, tens of thousands of bitches are spayed every week without any complications at all, so it is, generally speaking, a very safe operation. Moreover, the benefits greatly outweigh the risks.

Joe's Surgery Casebook

A few months after I qualified as a vet, I experienced the nightmare case that all vets dread – the bitch spay that bled. It was probably the third or fourth time I'd done the operation on my own. The patient was a large Golden Retriever (whose name escapes me now – or perhaps I've blanked it from my memory!). The operation itself seemed to go well, and I was pleased to see her sitting up in her kennel soon after I'd finished as this is usually a sign that all is well.

However, it wasn't long before my initial satisfaction and confidence turned to panic. A couple of hours later when the dog had just been picked up to go home, the owner rushed back into the surgery and said that the dog was bleeding heavily all over the back seat of her car. My heart skipped several beats and I felt suddenly sick with worry, which only worsened when I saw the dog being carried back into the surgery – bright-red blood was dripping copiously from her spay wound and she looked weak and very dull.

For a few seconds I was almost paralysed by fear, before forcing myself into action. I knew that the only possible hope for this dog was a second operation to locate and tie off the bleeding ovarian stump, which was almost certainly causing the bleeding. But there was very little time, as heavy bleeding like this can be life-threatening in minutes, so I called for assistance and took her straight back through to the operating theatre.

Once I'd put her on intravenous fluids to try to replace the volume of fluid in her circulation, I administered an anaesthetic, scrubbed up again, and undid the sutures to reopen the spay incision. Inside, her abdomen was awash with blood that spilled out on to the surgery floor, and made finding the source of the bleeding very difficult.

Thankfully, however, after a few frantic minutes, I managed to place a surgical clamp on the bleeding artery, and then tie a new catgut ligature around the base of the artery and stop the bleeding. She was still alive, but only just – and the next 24 hours would be critical as, after this quantity of blood loss, her prognosis would be very much in the balance.

After closing the wound for a second time, I placed her carefully in a recovery kennel and breathed a sigh of relief which I fervently hoped wasn't premature. That night I barely slept a wink, and rushed back to the surgery the following morning, not sure if I would find her alive or dead (this was back in the days before routine 24-hour hospitals were the norm, certainly in north Devon). My heart has rarely raced as it did when I opened the kennel-room door and looked down at my patient. For a second my heart sank as she appeared entirely still, but then she looked up, and, to my immense relief, she sat up and wagged her tail.

Despite the severity of the bleeding, she went on to make a full recovery. This case certainly taught me a lesson I'll never forget and made me always take the spaying operation seriously.

Having outlined the two operations, it's time to consider why we neuter our pets, the advantages and disadvantages, and how it fits into our philosophy of living with our dogs. Firstly, let's take castrating male dogs. The main reasons for carrying out this surgery are:

- Preventing reproduction and therefore reducing dog populations and unwanted litters
- Reducing behavioural traits linked to testosterone – aggression, wanderlust, urine marking, inappropriate sexual behaviour (eg leg humping!)
- Preventing health problems linked to male animals – testicular cancer, prostate disease

These are all good reasons and any one of them would justify the procedure – and in most cases two or more are relevant. Neutered male dogs tend to be less aggressive and better behaved. There is also a view that they are likely to live longer because, by reducing the physical and emotional stresses that sexual hormones induce, the body is likely to last a little longer. These effects are more pronounced the earlier you carry out the procedure, as behavioural traits in particular tend to become ingrained if castration is left too long, and removing the cause of the behaviour (testosterone) doesn't then always remove the behaviour itself.

Arguments against castration on the other hand (apart from the obvious one of preventing reproduction in dogs that are wanted to sire litters!) include:

- Change of character
- Change in coat and appearance
- Increased tendency to put on weight
- Surgical risks
- Moral argument against 'emasculation' of a male animal

These arguments all carry some validity and need to be taken into consideration – but, in my view, none of them is strong enough to sway the average dog owner away from having the operation done.

The change in character argument is the easiest to tackle as, apart from the impact of losing overtly male characteristics such as dominance, castration has little or no impact on the actual character of the dog. Character is formed by many factors, including genetics and external influences such as upbringing and environment, and sexual hormones only play a peripheral role. Therefore, there is no need to worry that castrating your dog will affect his underlying character – it might make him less headstrong, or less prone to bark at the postman, but it's not going to change who he is.

Change in coat is more of a real issue as testosterone does have an influence on the condition of the coat of male dogs, when neutering can lead to a once sleek and wiry coat becoming softer and fluffier. This is not a significant issue for most dog owners, but, if your dogs are destined for the show ring, you may need to think about the impact of neutering on the appearance of your dog (although personally I believe your priorities should be with the health of your dog, not its looks).

The argument that castration leads to weight gain is both true and false. It's true in that castration usually lowers the body's requirement for energy and, therefore, if you feed a neutered animal the same rations he was receiving before the operation, he is likely to put on weight. However, it's false because there's a simple solution to avoid this weight gain – feed less after the operation! It really is that straightforward and most vets would recommend dropping the calorific intake of a neutered dog by around 20 per cent compared to their ration before the operation, and this should maintain the dog at a stable weight (and even save you money on food bills!). You can get diets specifically designed for neutered dogs, or you can use 'light' foods which have fewer calories than regular diets – or simply feed 20 per cent less volume of your dog's normal food. Obviously the 20 per cent figure is only a rough guide and you need to apply the condition-scoring assessment we discussed previously to ensure you are feeding the correct amount.

The penultimate argument against castration is probably the easiest to deal with – surgical risk. As mentioned elsewhere, the castration operation is very low risk in the vast majority of cases (with the exception of the cryptorchid operation) and there is no way that a tiny risk of complication should be a deciding factor in whether or not you have a dog castrated. I have carried out thousands of these operations in my career and never had a significant problem. Apart from the occasional wound infection or swollen scrotum post-operatively, I've never seen a problematic operation undertaken by a colleague either – so it really is not something to worry about.

And that brings us on to the final argument, that of moral objections against castration. This is where things get a little less clear cut and the arguments become more emotive. The main arguments used by opponents to castration on moral grounds are that it is a breach of trust between the dog and owner (as the owner has undertaken to do what is best for the dog not what is most convenient for the owner); that it is cruel and unnecessary; and that, because it is unacceptable in humans, it is unacceptable in dogs.

I think the crux of this objection is whether or not we differentiate ourselves from dogs and accept that moral decisions do not necessarily apply to each species in the same way. Personally, I think it is clear that morals apply to dogs and people in different ways and that dogs do not require the same ethical protection as people. If this was not the case, we would surely have to argue that putting dogs on leads or putting them in kennels, or forcing them to have vaccinations would also constitute infringements of a dog's moral rights. In fact, if you take this argument to its logical conclusion, one could conclude that we have no moral right to keep dogs as pets at all and we have no moral right to keep any domestic animals under our dominion. This is clearly (in my view anyway) a nonsensical position, as human society has been built on the foundations of our moral and intellectual superiority to animals and I can't see how we can operate a society on any other basis. If we were to abandon this position, then we would be unable to eat meat, dairy products or eggs, keep pets, build houses (as they impact on animal habitat) or conduct the vast majority of the activities on which our society is built.

So, like it or not, we are born into a world where we have a responsibility to care for the other species on the planet, but not a duty to treat them as equals. This might sound harsh, but remember that I'm not suggesting that this should give us carte blanche to treat animals in any way we see fit – far from it. I believe that we, as the superior species on the planet, are in a unique position to safeguard our fellow inhabitants, and, to do this, we have to accept and use our intelligence and morals to do what we believe is best for our animal companions. In the case of castration, to end a rather long-winded, but necessary discussion, I think the moral case is clear for us to neuter animals for their own good and for the good of their position in a human-dominated world. I hope that makes sense!

I hope I have persuaded you that castration is a sensible procedure for the vast majority of dogs, and there are very few good reasons not to have it done, unless you are planning to breed from your dog.

The final point to discuss before we move on to the pros and cons of spaying female dogs is the timing of the castration operation. In the UK it is traditionally carried out from six months of age, but in some rescue centres around the world it is undertaken on dogs as young as three months old. Generally speaking, the earlier the operation is done, the more pronounced its effects on the dog in terms of behaviour, character and physical make-up, so, if you are keen to have a placid, gentle dog, and you're not worried about some 'feminisation' of features such as less pronounced musculature and a fluffier coat, then I would suggest there is no need to wait beyond the first opportunity at six months of age.

If, however, you would prefer your dog to become slightly more masculine in looks and character, then you could wait until he is a little older – perhaps around 12 months of age – before having him done.

Moving on, it is now the turn of the female neutering operation to come under scrutiny and here there are stronger arguments on both sides of the fence. The main arguments in favour of spaying are as follows:
- Preventing reproduction and therefore reducing dog populations and unwanted litters
- Prevention of several serious health problems – mammary cancer and womb infections (pyometra)
- Prevention of seasons

The 'anti' arguments include:
- Surgical risk
- Increased risk of urinary incontinence
- Change to character
- Change to appearance

• Increased tendency for weight gain
• Moral arguments

Let's consider the 'pro' arguments first, which are reasonably simple and clear cut. In addition to the obvious population-control benefit, there is a clear and unequivocal health benefit to the dog; spaying a female dog before her second season will protect her absolutely against mammary cancer and pyometra, both of which are life-threatening conditions that are relatively common in older bitches. This is the main argument in favour of neutering female dogs, and it is a hard one to refute as the health benefits are so clear and positive.

The last argument for spaying is the weakest – spaying obviously prevents seasons, regular episodes which can cause discomfort for the dog, inconvenience for the owner and behavioural problems for male dogs in the neighbourhood! As I said, it's not a great argument, but one that's worth considering when making this important decision.

Some of the arguments against spaying are similar to those against castration, and, for the character, appearance and weight-gain arguments, I would refer you to the previous discussion of these points under castration.

The more important points to consider are the issues of surgical risk and increased risk of urinary incontinence. Surgical risk is something we've already looked at in detail, and, although the risks are undoubtedly higher than for male dogs, they are still nowhere near significant enough to represent a serious reason for not having a bitch spayed – the positives of the health benefits easily outweigh the minimal risk of the surgery in almost all cases.

The case for the urinary incontinence argument requires more consideration, as, if neutering does increase the possibility of a dog losing control of their bladder later in life, as some evidence would seem to suggest, this would be a significant issue. The theory is that by neutering bitches we remove the main source of oestrogen, and a low level of this female hormone is implicated in some cases of urinary incontinence in older bitches. However, a firm link between neutering and urinary incontinence has never been satisfactorily established and the general consensus in the veterinary community is that the effect is minimal if present at all. Most vets would agree that the definite, proven benefits of the operation in preventing mammary cancer and pyometra far outweigh an unproven potential link with urinary incontinence, which while being obviously unpleasant is not a truly serious or life-threatening condition.

Joe's Surgery Casebook

NEUTERING IN AFRICA

As I write this book I've just returned from an amazing trip to Malawi in southern Africa where I spent a week working with a local animal charity, the LSPCA, helping with vaccination and neutering clinics in impoverished townships close to the capital city Lilongwe.

The vaccination clinics, where we inoculated thousands of

chickens against a respiratory disease, and hundreds of dogs against rabies, were fascinating and introduced me to working in such an alien environment compared to the luxury of my surgery in the UK. But it was at the neutering clinics that my eyes were well and truly opened to the immense challenges faced by the vets in situations like this.

The operating facilities were as far from the clean operating theatres we take for granted in the developed world as you can imagine – all we had was a flimsy tent, a few rickety tables and rolled-up towels in place of surgical cradles to hold our patients in position. Nothing was sterile, including the instruments which were simply washed between operations (they would always be sterilised in an autoclave at home). The swirling wind blew dust into every corner of the clinic. The dogs were anaesthetised using a very basic injectable combination that gave unpredictable results – and led to several dogs waking up mid-operation and requiring emergency top-ups – and they recovered after their surgery on dusty blankets before being taken home to recover in rusty old wheelbarrows.

It was so far removed from everything I was used to back in the UK, but it certainly taught me to be quick and efficient with my surgery – and to really value the facilities we have at home. Our patients don't know how lucky they are!

TRAINING

The main building block of any successful relationship with a dog is training. Without instruction, a dog will always struggle to fit into our human world, and behavioural problems will invariably arise. One of our primary responsibilities as dog owners is to be teachers – schooling our companions in the ways of the world and helping them to grow up into mature, well-behaved and sociable members of our society. A suitable and appropriate training regime helps to build and deepen your bond with your dog, and is the cornerstone of a happy life together.

If we take a slightly more scientific look at the effects of successfully training a dog, we can identify five key benefits:

- Provides a foundation for successful communication between owner and dog
- Builds confidence and trust – on both sides
- Promotes affection, relaxation and wellbeing
- Improves the dog's attention and concentration
- Provides the owner with effective management tools

Without training – and therefore without these five benefits – you cannot hope to have a fulfilling life together with your dog. Training is absolutely fundamental to a healthy relationship with your dog, and getting it right during this crucial period in your dog's development is one of the most important things you can do for your dog – and yourself.

With the benefits of training established, let's start thinking about the practical aspects of training your dog. If you read and believe many training books and manuals, you'd be forgiven for thinking that this is a really complex and difficult task, involving detailed theories and complex training regimes. But my philosophy on this subject is much simpler and I believe will allow you to achieve results that are as good as, if not better than, the most comprehensive and involved training techniques.

In my view, training all comes down to one simple goal – building the right relationship between owner and dog. Get this right and training will come as naturally as breathing – but get it wrong and no amount of expensive canine therapy will rescue you and your dog from the problems that will undoubtedly ensue. So what is a 'healthy relationship' between dog and owner? Well, it's really very simple, and can be summarised by my three 'R's of relationship: respect, reward and repeat.

Respect is the real cornerstone of relationship building with your dog and it's a two-way process. It is absolutely vital that there is mutual respect between you – but also key that this respect is not equal or the same. If that sounds confusing, let me elaborate. Dogs and people are different and have different roles in the owner–pet relationship and within the family which must be reflected in the balance of respect between owner and dog. You need to respect your dog for who he is, respect his needs, his desires and his freedoms, whereas your dog needs to respect you for what you are – leader, role model, mentor and, ultimately, master.

Master is one of those words that seems old-fashioned in the context of modern dog training, and will no doubt have the politically correct dog-training establishment (yes, such a thing does exist!) up in arms but I make no apologies for using it. At the end of the day we are deluding ourselves if we try to build a relationship with a dog in any other way than based around the concept of respect from dog to master. Think of the best-trained dogs you know and what springs to mind – sheepdogs working to the whistle of their master on the moors, police dogs controlling their aggression until instructed to unleash it by their handler, show dogs trotting obediently around the ring behind their master – the list goes on, and each example has one thing in common: well-trained dogs have strong, hierarchical relationships with their masters.

Being master of a dog does not mean being a dictator or tyrant, it simply means that underpinning your relationship is a hierarchy with you possessing ultimate dominance over your dog. Having dominance does not give the master a licence to mistreat or exploit their dog – far from it; the role of head of the pack carries with it very great responsibilities, with the wellbeing of the rest of the pack in your hands.

The origins of this aspect of our relationship with our dogs come from the social structure of the wild dog pack, which is highly hierarchical with clear dominant and submissive members. This structure developed in the wild with the simple purpose of minimising conflict within a social group. By having a clear pecking order, with every dog knowing their place, the pack has inherent order and discipline, with disputes far less frequent than if the pack was simply an actual 'dog-eat-dog' world. After millennia of evolution, this hierarchical structure is hardwired into the brains of all dogs, even our artificially selected modern domestic pets, and it is the underlying reason why we have to build an effective master–dog relationship. In the eyes of our dogs, our families are packs, and they have an inherent need to know where everyone stands in the social order. If this isn't clear, then the dog will be confused and conflict will arise as the dog struggles to understand their place in the pack.

It might sound cruel to treat a dog as subservient, but in fact not establishing this relationship is far crueller. Dogs are only happy in a stable social setting where they know where everybody stands – take this structure away from them and you set their feet on social quicksand, taking away the stability they need to form healthy relationships.

Despite the clear and simple science behind this view of canine relationships, there are many in the behaviour and training worlds who feel that we need to move away from this model and adopt a more consensual approach to our relationships with dogs. Talk to many modern trainers and they will explain how you achieve amazing results through mutual respect and understanding and without the need to resort to a master-and-dog-style relationship – but I think their theories just don't add up and they are driven more by emotion than science. It is all too easy to view hierarchical relationships as bad – we are taught to view all humans as equals, so it is understandable that some people feel the need to extend this equality to our canine companions. But to do so is to misunderstand the basic nature of our relationship with dogs, and, as I explained in the previous section on neutering, we have to accept – and celebrate – the differences between our species if we are to build healthy, long-term relationships between them. To enforce a blanket philosophy of equality is not only nonsensical, it is also damaging and disrespectful towards the animals who share our lives. Dogs have no concept of equality or fairness, and why should we force them to live by these very human ethics? Instead, isn't it fairer for us to build our relationships with animals on their terms, not ours? Dogs understand the pack structure – they don't understand human society – and, if we are to have dogs as domestic companions, the very least we can do is let them live by their rules and not force them to adopt ours.

So don't be swayed by modern theories that are based more on us rather than our dogs – and remember that a happy dog is one that lives by dog rules!

After respect comes reward and this is the second key facet of building a healthy relationship with your dog and therefore allowing you to train your dog successfully. Communication is vital when building any relationship, and the primary language understood by both dogs and people is the language of reward. Reward – or the lack of one – can be a surprisingly flexible language, allowing detailed communication between you and your dog. The type of reward and the context and timing of its appearance are the vocabulary that make up the language of reward. By learning to understand the subtleties of these words, it's amazing how detailed your communication with your dog can become. With the right words in this language, you can express your pleasure and your disappointment; you can build expectations and hold attention; you can teach and you can discipline.

The nature of the rewards themselves can vary enormously, from edible treats to attention or toys, and there are many different schools of training that exploit these differing rewards.

CLICKER TRAINING

The click of a tiny plastic device may sound like an unlikely reward for a dog, but the principle behind clicker training is very simple – and remarkably effective. The theory goes back to the famous Russian physiologist Petrovich Pavlov and his drooling dogs. Pavlov showed that dogs accustomed to hearing a certain sound such as the ticking of a metronome while they ate their food would salivate at the sound of the ticking whether or not the food was present. This principle of creating associations in the brain that link a stimuli such as a sound with a feeling or reaction is known as classical conditioning and is the basis for clicker training.

With clicker training the dog is conditioned to associate the sound of the clicker with a positive event or reward such as a treat or attention. This is achieved by clicking the clicker every time the dog receives the reward and, in time, the dog becomes so accustomed to the link between the reward and the click that he becomes conditioned and the positive sensations linked to the reward become permanently associated with the click. From then on, whenever the dog hears the click he gets the same positive feeling as if he'd had the reward itself and the click can be used in place of the reward to communicate with the dog.

The advantages of clicker conditioning your dog is that it allows you to communicate with your dog without continually giving actual physical rewards (which can be a problem if they are food based) and it also allows much more accurate and consistent communication. In many cases, the human voice is too variable, or a treat delivered too long after an action for a dog to clearly understand what they are being rewarded for. The clicker delivers an instant message of reward and can be delivered at precisely the right time so the dog knows exactly what they've done right.

Whether you choose one type of reward or a combination, you have to make sure it's appropriate for your dog. There's no point trying to communicate with your dog using tit-bits if he is a picky eater with little interest in food, or using a toy when all your dog really wants is a nibble of sausage. By the time your dog has reached adolescence, you should have a deep enough understanding of his character, desires and dislikes to be able to select the most appropriate reward, but, if it isn't clear to you what motivates your dog, a little trial and error is the best way to find out what really gets him going – and, believe me, there's always something for every dog. You may think that your obstinate Jack Russell Terrier is completely un-trainable because he turns his nose up at treats and walks away from a ball – but dig a little deeper and you may find that what really drives him is something simple like a scratch behind the ear or a few affectionate words.

The third 'R' of my relationship-building philosophy is repeat, and this is really the engine that drives the formation of the relationship. Dogs, whether we like it or not, are relatively simple animals with minds that are easily distracted, and repetition of instruction and communication is vital if they are to understand and remember what they are being taught. You might think it is harsh to describe a dog as 'simple' and I'm sure the PC training brigade are bristling with indignation once again, but the fact is dogs really are relatively simple compared to us. They don't have the mental capacity for abstract thought, or the self-awareness required to motivate learning – they have minds that have evolved perfectly to suit their particular needs, with practical skills and undoubted, but limited, emotions that equipped them to survive in the wild and work to build families and simple communities of packs. A dog cannot decide that he wants to learn how to sit and then focus on the task in hand, any more than you or I can follow a scent for miles, and it is one of the challenges of building a relationship and training a dog that we have to work with his limitations (and our own as well!).

Joe's Surgery Casebook

A RELATIONSHIP ON THE ROCKS

When Mrs Potter first brought her Cocker Spaniel puppy Lucy into the surgery I could tell there was going to be trouble. It was clear from that first day when Lucy was only eight weeks old that there was only one boss in this relationship, and it wasn't Mrs Potter. Lucy barked and Mrs Potter jumped to attention, lavishing attention and rewards on her beloved new friend, and when she squealed and turned to nip at me when I gave her her vaccination, Mrs Potter reacted with a cry of distress followed by an emotional 'good girl' and lavish cuddle. I sighed and tried my best to explain that this kind of subservience on her part would only lead to trouble for both of them in the long run, but my advice was clearly falling on deaf ears.

Over the next year Lucy was a regular visitor to the surgery, for her routine vaccinations, worming and neutering, plus the occasional visits for ear infections and once to remove a grass seed from her paw. And on each occasion Lucy's behaviour seemed worse than before. She grew from a playful puppy to a nervous and unpredictable adolescent and eventually into a downright unpleasant adult dog who would even turn on her besotted owner.

'I just don't know what to do with her,' moaned Mrs Potter on her most recent visit after I'd struggled to muzzle her for her vaccinations, 'she's lovely most of the time but sometimes she can just be a real terror.'

I explained, for the nth time, how her continual pampering, inconsistent discipline and inappropriate rewards were leading to Lucy's problems. With no clear hierarchy between Mrs Potter and Lucy, it was obvious why the dog was so badly behaved. Without a radical change on Mrs Potter's part, I couldn't see how the situation could possibly be resolved.

In the end Mrs Potter ended up being forced to offer Lucy up for rehoming at the local animal shelter. It was a very sad end to a failed relationship, and just goes to show how crucial it is to build a proper relationship around the dog's rules, not our emotions. I just hope that Lucy found herself a more disciplined owner who managed to rescue her and rebuild her confidence in people which is the only way she can hope to lead a happy life in the human world.

Repetition is the key driver of learning in the wild – a dog learns how to track and hunt successfully by the consistent repetition of his environment in rewarding his successes and punishing his failures. A dog that doesn't slink low to their haunches when stalking their quarry will fail more often than they succeed, and this will be repeated until the dog learns their lesson, just as a growing puppy will learn by repetition of mistakes and successes how to socialise with the other dogs in their pack.

In the domestic environment, we use repetition to

communicate our messages loud, clear and, above all, consistent. It may seem slow and laborious initially to have to repeat ourselves over and over again, but, despite my early words about dogs being simple, they are quick learners and in many cases a few repetitions of a message are all that's required. The problems arise when a message isn't repeated consistently and a dog becomes confused. For example, if one day you tell your dog to sit and you wait until he obeys and give him a reward, but the next day you tell him to sit but don't bother to finish the process by waiting for him to comply and rewarding him, he will become confused: Am I supposed to sit when he says that word, or not?

Repetition is reinforcement and it should be used together with reward to communicate with your dog. Decide on your message, select the correct reward and repeat consistently until it's become second nature to your dog – easy!

With the basics of relationship building established, it's time to think about how this translates into effective, practical training.

Training is a gradual process that can't be rushed and doesn't always bring instant rewards – it requires patience and perseverance. And you also need to be methodical and work to a plan; there's no point trying to teach a dog to shake hands before you've mastered the sit command for example. And you need to allow your dog to learn at his own pace – if you rush him or try to work on too many commands at once, you'll end up achieving nothing more than confusing your dog, and that's a one-way ticket to behavioural problems!

Before we look at the details of specific training programmes, it's worth understanding that all training comes down to the same process, built on the three 'R's we've established as the cornerstones of your relationship with your dog – respect, reward and repeat. Respect is not so much a part of training, but more of an underlying factor that must be present if reward and repeat are going to work properly. But how do you deliver respect? We've talked about the theory of dominance and pack culture, but how does that translate into practical actions that will ensure that your dog has a clear understanding of his position in the family pack and of your role as his master and mentor?

Establishing dominance is not about beating your dog into physical submission – far from it. If you build your relationship from an early age, there should never be any need to resort to physical means to enforce your dominance, and there is never an excuse for mistreating your dog under the guise of expressing your dominance. Dominance is all about reducing physical conflict and can easily be established and maintained without any need for physical intimidation. In fact, probably a better term than dominance, which carries with it so many negative connotations related to physical control, is 'benevolent dominance' which better describes the concept of being in charge, but doing it nicely, which is at the heart of my philosophy.

The fundamental key to establishing this position of benevolent dominance is a state of mind on your part. You need to be comfortable with the role of head of the pack and, once you have that in your mind, your actions will follow automatically, as your dog will be able to read them and understand the message you are delivering. Try to free your mind from the constraints of human society and think in terms of your dog's psychology rather than your own. He needs to see you as a decisive and consistent leader, and, to achieve that, you need to think in that way whenever you are interacting with your dog.

Being decisive and consistent does not mean you can't play with your dog or indulge yourself in games and the general fun of interacting with a young dog – but it does mean that you have to do so on your terms, not your dog's. For example, you need to initiate periods of play, and bring them to an end, you need to bring the toys to the game and take them away at the end, and you need to win any games with a competitive edge such as tug of war. By playing in this way, your dog will clearly understand that it is you who is in charge, and they will accept that without any need on your part to enforce your position with any kind of physical actions.

Other ways in which you can impress on your dog the hierarchy of the family pack include simple but effective techniques such as eating before you feed your dog, passing through doors in front of your dog, and practising taking food and toys away from your dog. All of these actions will serve to reinforce in your dog his relative submission to you and, once that position is established in his mind, you will have taken the first and most important step towards building a healthy relationship with your dog which will allow you to train him successfully.

With respect established, you can start to mould your dog's character and behaviour by training to suit your lifestyle. As previously mentioned, training takes time and patience, and you need to go about it in a logical and methodical manner – but, before we get on to the details of a training plan, it's worth a quick word on the science behind the techniques we use to implement training regimes.

Training is learning, and there are two basic forms of learning – classical conditioning and operant conditioning. Classical conditioning, as mentioned in the discussion on clicker training, is the process by which the mind links two stimuli (sense impressions), for example the smell of food with the subsequent taste of the meal, or the sound of a click with the reward of the treat. Operant conditioning on the other hand is the association between an 'operation' or stimulus that we control and a response. A typical example would be the way in which a dog learns that carrying his lead and dropping it at your feet has the consequence of initiating a walk or that going to the toilet outside leads to a reward.

Most learning experiences combine both classical and operant conditioning, and, while these theories are probably not going to be at the forefront of your mind while you are putting a training regime into practice, it is useful to understand them, particularly so when things don't go to plan and you are faced with dealing with undesirable behaviours, of which more later on. But, for now, let's get back to training, and what follows is my suggestion for a routine training schedule for an adolescent dog:

STEP 1: ATTENTION!

Teaching a dog to pay attention might sound obvious and may well come naturally to some dogs, but for others you may need to work a little on the basic idea that your dog needs to pay attention to what you are doing and saying. Some dogs are easily distracted, and need training to help them understand how to focus on you, as, without this ability, you are going to struggle to teach your dog anything at all. Teaching a dog to pay attention is also an opportunity to make sure they understand the one simple word you're going to use more than any other in their training programme – their name. By associating the practice of paying attention with the sound of their name, you will have a head start when it comes to more involved commands, such as recall, which usually involve calling your dog by name.

It's easy to do – all you need to do is use your selected reward to hold their attention while continuing to give them your attention, repeating their name and maintaining eye contact. So, if you are using food as a reward, introduce the treat to your dog and then hold it in front of your face as you look at him and repeat his name clearly before giving him the treat and a verbal reinforcement of his good behaviour (such as 'good dog!'). If his attention wanders, then there's no reward, and gradually you'll be able to extend the period of time you hold his attention for until you can dispense with the reward altogether and your dog will have come to associate paying attention to you – and hearing his name – with the positive sensation of the reward. In other words, you will have classically conditioned him to enjoy paying attention to you.

STEP 2: SIT!

Teaching your dog to sit is the basic command that he needs to learn, and is an essential part of his training process. Without this basic command being reliably obeyed, you cannot hope to have an obedient dog – and as it is such a ubiquitous command that is used not just by you, the dog's owner, but also by many other people in your dog's life, not obeying it properly can be more of an issue than simply causing problems when you need your dog to sit down. If your dog gets into the habit of consistently disobeying the sit command as he's likely to do if not trained to obey it (as he's unlikely to be able to avoid it), then he will start to question the necessity of obeying other commands and your authority over him will be undermined. Repetition is a powerful tool in training but it can also inadvertently become just as powerful a tool in undoing all your good work if you aren't careful.

Teaching the sit command is thankfully very easy, as it's such a natural thing to do, and it usually only takes a few sessions for your dog to get the hang of it. The theory behind the technique I use is called 'lure training'. It is simply the process of conditioning a behaviour that you lure your dog into performing – so you get him to sit by physically manipulating him into performing the action, and then reward him as soon as he does it. The result is that via the learning process of operant conditioning your dog will have associated the operation of sitting with the positive reward stimulus of a treat.

To achieve this, all you need to do is establish eye contact with your dog and hold his attention with a treat or toy, and then, while giving the 'sit' command, move the reward upwards and backwards above his head. In following the treat or toy, your dog will naturally move into the sitting position, and, as soon as his bottom touches the ground, give him the reward and plenty of praise. If you're doing clicker training, then, as soon as his bottom touches the ground, give him a click so he knows exactly what he's done that's right.

It really is that easy and most dogs will quickly understand what's required of them when they hear the sit command. Once you've communicated what you expect of your dog, make sure you follow the third 'R' and repeat, repeat and repeat some more – there's no such thing as over-reinforcing a basic behaviour such as sit. The more you go through the process and reward correct compliance again and again, the more ingrained the training will become, which is crucial if you're going to be able to rely on it in difficult and stressful situations later in life.

STEP 3: STAY AND COME

With the sit command under your belt, it's time to move on to the logical next step – the stay and come commands. As well as being essential commands for a well-behaved dog, they also establish your authority over your dog at a distance, something which is important if you are going to control your dog outside the house.

To teach the stay command, firstly tell your dog to sit and, with him in this position, hold his attention with a finger raised in front of your face. And then, while firmly giving the 'stay' command', move backwards slowly, all the while maintaining eye contact. After holding him in the sitting position for a short period – probably only a few seconds initially – give the 'come' command and give him his reward when he reaches you. If he disobeys, by wandering off or coming to you before you give the 'come' command, simply walk away without rewarding him with a treat or even attention. There is no need to admonish him or tell him off, as simply not getting his reward gives a clear enough signal that he has not behaved correctly. In fact, the act of telling him off can be counterproductive as it constitutes giving attention which some dogs will interpret as a reward even if the attention is intended to be negative. You may also confuse the dog by overtly punishing him when he may have been quite close to doing what was required: he may have understood the concept of 'come' but not quite worked out the 'stay' bit, and, if you punish him for coming to you too soon, you may just serve to undermine his understanding of the one part of the training he'd just got his head around!

Once your dog has mastered a short stay and come sequence, it's simply a case of extending the stay interval and increasing the distance from you to the dog. This should be done gradually, and again without negative input when he gets it wrong. Although the idea of dominance-based training may suggest punishment, that is not the case at all – your dominance over your dog simply gives you the right, in their eyes, to give commands. How you teach these commands is a separate issue and positive rewards are not only more pleasant for all concerned than punishments, they also happen to be far more effective. It is much easier to clearly associate a specific action with a reward than it is an action with a punishment, which often comes after the action has finished and simply confuses the dog who doesn't know why they've been punished. Rewards, given at the right time, are by far and away the most effective form of training communication, and negative tactics such as a raised voice or angry tone of voice should be reserved for specific occurrences where a clear and specific transgression of a well-established rule or command has taken place.

STEP 3: RECALL

Recall differs from stay and come in that it is used in situations where you haven't previously held your dog's attention and told them to stay. The recall command needs to work in any situation, no matter what distractions might be present, and no matter what the starting point in terms of distance and activity. If you're going to be able to lead a fulfilling life with your dog, including off-the-lead exercise, then being able to reliably call your dog back to you no matter what the situation is essential. The number of dogs who end up living miserable existences with no access to free-running exercise simply because they have not been trained to come back reliably is a depressing testament to the failure of so many dog-training programmes.

The command used to initiate the recall action is generally based around the dog's name. For example, my dog Jack responds to a bellowed 'Jaaack!' or a more formal 'Jack, come here!' It doesn't really matter what the actual word that is used is, as long as you are consistent, at least to begin with. Once your dog has got the hang of coming back to you at the sound of your voice, they will usually respond to any word, relying more on your tone of voice and the body language than on the specific word itself. I have experimented with Jack, and discovered that I can shout pretty much anything that sounds remotely like his name, or even a completely unrelated word as long as I do so in the same tone of voice and with the intonation that I use when I call his name. So if you're in the Cotswolds and you hear a male voice bellowing out 'Trouser Press!' or 'Chicken Soup', don't worry – it's just me testing the limits of Jack's recall ability!

Teaching the recall command uses a slightly different method of skill learning compared to the sit and stay commands, that of 'behaviour capture'. This is the simple process by which you wait until the dog performs the action you are aiming to teach, and then reward him for doing so – you're not inducing the behaviour, just waiting for it to happen naturally and then conditioning your dog to associate the command, action and positive stimulus of reward. Therefore, the way to start teaching the recall command is not to try to initiate the action with your command, as you'll invariably fail, but to give the command once your dog is already coming back to you – and 'capture' this desirable behaviour. This might all sound odd, as you're not actually telling your dog what to do, but that's not the point – what you are achieving by giving the command while he is running back to you of his own accord is starting to condition him to the association between the command and the action of running back to you. When he gets back to you, reward him with a treat, toy or click, and you reinforce the association between command, action and a positive reward.

Over time, with much repetition, your dog will become so accustomed to the link between your command with the action of running back to you and the pleasure of the reward at the end of it that, when he eventually hears the command at a time when he is not already running back to you, he will almost automatically turn and come back to you. This is clever training – harnessing the power of operant and classical conditioning to teach your dog a command without his even knowing what you are doing!

Before moving on to the next step in my training programme, it's worth mentioning one of the main pitfalls that dog owners often fall into when teaching the recall command. The issue arises when a disobedient dog disappears off into the distance and, despite your constant calling, refuses to come back to you. And then, when he does, finally, come back covered in mud and brambles from his adventures, wagging his tail, you do what seems to come naturally in this situation and tell him off for his gross disobedience.

There are two classic errors in this scenario, both of which can do irreparable damage to recall training. The first is to continue to call your dog when they are clearly not going to obey. In this situation, all you will achieve by continuing to give your command is to subconsciously associate the command with the action of disobeying it in your dog's mind – and unsurprisingly this will not do your chances of teaching your dog to obey the command any good at all. And the second mistake is to greet your errant dog with a telling off when he belatedly comes back to you. Think about this situation from your dog's point of view – he's been off, had a fun adventure and then does what all good dogs do, and come back to his master – but, instead of the praise and reward he's expecting for coming back to you, he gets a telling off instead which is most confusing and makes him think twice about coming back at all the next time he's out and about.

So remember the two golden rules of teaching recall:

1. Only use the recall command when you are confident that it will be obeyed – never use it in a lost-cause situation when your dog is clearly not going to come back or you will simply undermine its effectiveness.

2. Always praise and reward your dog for coming back to you – no matter how disobedient they've been beforehand. Dogs always associate your response with the here and now rather than with their past behaviour.

STEP 4: WALKING ON A LEAD

In a way, this could come before step three, but personally I view recall as a far more important command to teach than walking on a lead, so, although it may be more logical to teach this before you get out into the park or the fields and practise your recall, I am putting it after recall to reflect the relative priority of the two commands.

Walking well on a lead is a useful skill to teach your dog, and will make both of your lives an awful lot easier than having to deal with a poorly behaved animal. Dogs who are not taught how to walk properly by your side on a lead are more likely to pull at the lead and act unpredictably, which can be dangerous as well as annoying. Dogs who pull and yank on the lead can end up causing you more than just a strained arm – they are much more of a danger near roads and around other people and there have been many accidents involving dogs who lurch out into the road from the pavement despite being on the lead.

So it's important to teach your dog how to behave correctly on the lead – but it's not always as easy as it might sound. Being restrained on a lead is an alien concept for a dog, and one that doesn't fit neatly into behaviours that have long evolutionary roots heading back to their wild origins as commands such as sit and stay do (being commanded to stay in one place and then move by the dominant dog is an essential part of pack hunting). It's not just getting used to being restrained on the lead that your dog has to cope with, it's also walking by your side with the lead slack which must be mastered – a difficult concept if you think about it from the dog's perspective. Firstly you introduce me to this collar and lead which prevent me from going where I want – and then you expect me to walk by your side and not to explore the world up to the limits of the lead!

Getting your dog used to the idea of a lead needs to be approached gradually and with plenty of positive rewards. Your puppy should be happy with a collar from an early age, and the sooner you start lead training, the easier it will be for him to accept the idea of being controlled by what is effectively an extension of your arm! Simply and gradually build up his trust and acceptance by putting him on the lead and giving him positive rewards such as treats when he is calm. Don't play games or over-excite him – you want him to associate being on the lead with a calm state of behaviour, rather than thinking of it as an invitation to get excited.

Once he is happy with the feeling of being on the lead, you can use your newly acquired 'stay and come' commands to introduce him to the concept of following the lead without being dragged by it. This is an important step to get right as it's far easier to teach him at an early stage that a lead is a guideline not a rope for pulling at than try to re-educate him at a later date when he's already got used to being pulled by the lead.

You should gradually be able to accustom him to walking to you on the lead, and then walking next to you. It's worth mentioning at this stage that it really doesn't matter which side of you he walks on. If you want to do things by the book and conform to the standards of show rings and the Kennel Club, then your dog should be by your left-hand side, but there is absolutely no reason why this is the case. In my opinion, you should accustom your dog to being comfortable walking on either side of your body as there are bound to be circumstances when it will be useful for him to be on either side, such as when passing other dogs or avoiding cyclists.

Use rewards to keep your dog at your side when you walk – his nose should be level with your legs and, if he strays in front of you, stop and call him back to your side before continuing. In time, your dog will learn that walking calmly by your side leads to reward and the praise of his master, and repetition reinforces this association until it becomes second nature to walk in this way. Some people like to associate a command with this action, such as 'heel' and that is perfectly fine – although you could argue that there is no need for a command as the simple act of walking on the lead should be instruction enough to your dog.

Those are the four main elements of basic training, and you should concentrate on getting all four firmly established before considering moving on to more complex training routines.

FOUR

Living With
Your Dog

This chapter is really at the heart of the book and deals with your everyday interactions with your dog and how important these are for building and maintaining a strong and healthy relationship between you and your dog. You and your dog share your lives – there's no getting away from that fact – and you have to take that into consideration in every aspect of your life, from organising family time to working schedules and holidays. You cannot make a significant decision in your life without considering its potential impact on your dog as our domestic dogs are so completely reliant on their human families in every aspect of their lives, from food and shelter to exercise and healthcare. By taking on the role of owner – or master as perhaps we should refer to ourselves in this context – we take on responsibility for our dogs' lives, and therefore it is incumbent upon us to give careful consideration to the effect on the lives of our dogs at every turn of our own lives.

So what does this theory mean in practice? Well, I think the easiest approach is to take a look at the life of an average dog owner and see how each aspect of that life can impact on the owner's canine companions, as well as how some small changes in the owner's attitude and routine can help create a far more healthy life for both dog and owner.

Let's call this average dog owner Mr Smith, and let's imagine that Mr Smith is a 'Family Man' in our dog-owner classification, with a wife and two young children. The family dog is a Labrador called Rover and he's been with the family since puppyhood.

Every morning Mr Smith feeds Rover and then takes him out for a short walk in the local park before heading off to work. During the day Rover is left alone for long periods as Mrs Smith is also out at work and the children are at school. At 4pm the children and Mrs Smith return home and a busy period of eating and playing ensues before Mr Smith returns home and escapes the bedtime mêlée with another walk with Rover, before the dog settles down in front of the fire for the evening.

I think you'll agree that this is a pretty typical day in the life of a dog-owning family and contains within it all the major elements that we need to consider – feeding, walks, busy family time and time spent alone. So let's think about each of these elements that make up a typical day in the life of a dog-owning family in some more detail and see how each one can play an important role in the life of your dog.

FEEDING

Firstly let's consider feeding time. We've already talked a little about feeding schedules in the puppyhood chapter, but now we're discussing adult dogs it's worth revisiting this subject and thinking about how the frequency and timing of your dog's meals can play an important role in your relationship with him.

Food is one of the most important things in a dog's life, and, although I know there are plenty of dogs who pick at their food and don't appear to be that fussed about it, the fact remains that the vast majority of dogs live to eat and food is one of their main motivating desires. This is not surprising given their evolutionary background as scavenging hunters for whom food would have usually been scarce and highly prized. Food is the major commodity of wild dog packs and is far more than simply a source of sustenance – it is a currency, with great social meaning. The quantity and quality of food allocated to each dog in the pack helps to reinforce their social position in the group, and this is why dogs right up to this day attach great significance to every detail of their food. What your dog gets to eat, when he gets it and how he gets it are all important factors that will affect your dog more than you might imagine, and therefore it's important to have an understanding of these effects if you are to use them to communicate the right messages to your dog.

The first factor is what your dog eats. I'm not concerned here with the brand of pet food, or even whether you're feeding a commercial food or a home-prepared food. What is important is what your dog eats in relation to what you eat. In the wild dog pack that we know our dog's mind has been shaped by, the best parts of the carcass would be devoured by the dominant dogs, leaving the dogs at the lower end of the social spectrum to make do with the scraps left behind. Our domestic dogs need to be submissive to their human masters, as we have already established that this is one of the cornerstones of building a healthy relationship with your dog, and therefore they need to eat food that represents this status comparative to their owners. In practice, what this means is that it's important that you do not share your meals with your dog to any great extent. If your dog is aware that he is essentially eating at the high table of the pack, and getting the same food as his supposed social superiors, he is likely to become confused by the situation – and confusion is the enemy of good behaviour in the canine world.

So it's important to feed your dog his own food and not allow him to share yours. Whatever you decide to feed him, it should be from a separate source – perhaps kept in a different cupboard to your family food, or out in the shed – and clearly different in smell and character to the main family meals. The main exception I would give is for the occasional leftover to find its way into the dog's bowl as that is clearly a scrap from your table rather than a shared meal. Obviously there are health implications when it comes to feeding leftovers, particularly when it comes to overweight dogs, but all I'm concerned about here is the psychological effects of feeding, not the physical effects.

Having considered what to feed your dog, let's think about when to feed him as this is just as important and is another way in which your dog will pick up key messages from you that you might not even have been aware that you were giving. Just like the quality and quantity of food, timing of feeding communicates an important social message that has its origins in the evolution of pack structure. It's a generalisation to say that dominant animals feed before submissive ones, and that is the key fact to remember when thinking about when you feed your dog. If Mr Smith was to wake up, feed Rover and then immediately set about preparing breakfast for the rest of the family, Rover is going to subconsciously think, 'Hang on, if I'm eating first, does that mean I should be top dog in this pack?' If, on the other hand, Mr Smith waits until the rest of the family are eating their breakfast before considering Rover's food, then there will be no mixed messages and no confusion on the dog's part.

Finally on the subject of feeding comes the question of how to feed. This is probably the least important factor but it is still important nonetheless as the way and location in which you present the food will carry the same kind of subtle message to your dog that the type of food and timing of meals deliver. Never forget that dogs see the world in a very different way to how we do and that factors that might seem inconsequential to us, such as the type of dish or placement of a feeding station, might be of great importance to our dogs.

With how to feed, the issues to consider are what you feed the food in and where you feed him. On the first point,

I think the important fact to remember is that a dog should have a dedicated feeding bowl, so don't feed them from a dish used for your meals, and that the dish should be your property, not the dog's. So, after feeding, take the dish away and bring it out again only at feeding time as this will further reinforce the notion that you control your dog's feeding and he is reliant on you for delivery of his food. This again harks back to the situation in the wild whereby a submissive dog is completely reliant on the dominant dogs for their food – the dominant dogs will 'own' the carcass until giving it to the submissive dogs, and, by demonstrating control not only over the food itself but also the dish in which it always appears, you are further establishing your position relative to his. Again, please don't think I'm advocating an old school of dog behaviour where you have to be cruel to be kind – that is very far from my philosophy: my aim is to help you build a relationship that is based on foundations and rules that your dog understands and that sometimes might mean it seems out of touch with modern human society. Be that as it may, my priority is the welfare of dogs and I believe that basing our relationships on their societies rather than our own is the best way to achieve that goal.

Where you feed your dog is also important to consider as it too can deliver messages about status and dominance to your dog – albeit probably very subtle ones compared to some of the more blatant messages that we've discussed in relation to feeding. Just consider what various feeding locations might mean to your dog – and let's think back to the Smith family and Rover to illustrate this point again. If Mr Smith feeds

Rover next to the family table, then Rover is going to feel part of that high table of the social structure – not necessarily a problem if there is a clear dominance structure in place, but potentially undermining if the situation is less well established. However, if Rover gets his meals by the bins in the garden, is he going to feel like an outcast and perhaps not even a member of the family pack at all? I suspect that neither of these effects is quite as dramatic as this, but it is probably worth finding a solution somewhere between these two extremes that therefore avoids the potential for the wrong messages to be given to your dog. My dog Jack, for example, eats his meals just outside the back door (except if it's raining, of course) which makes it clear to him that he's not one of the social elite in the Inglis family – but that he is without question part of the family as well (however, given that Jack demolishes his food in about ten seconds flat, I'm not sure there's enough time for any such subtle messages to sink in!).

Like all aspects of dominance-pack theory, the idea that feeding plays a relevant role in modern dog–human relationships as I've described is often questioned and derided by dog behaviourists who adhere to other schools of thought – but, for me, I can't see how it couldn't be of some importance at the very least. We know that dogs are pack animals, and we know how important food and the timing of food are in the wild pack situation, so it would be incredible to believe that through a few thousand years of selective breeding we have managed to breed such an ingrained trait out of our modern dogs.

WALKS

Moving on from feeding in our day in the life of the Smith family and their faithful dog Rover, it's time to head out on a walk and think about what is probably the most important element of our lives with our dogs. With a few exceptions, dogs love walks, and walks represent in many ways the fundamental cornerstone of our relationship with them. How we walk, where we walk and what we do on our walks really goes to the heart of why we own dogs and what our relationship is with our dog. Obviously there are great differences between dog walks depending on the nature of individual dogs and breeds, as well as the circumstances of the owner, but underneath these differences lie some common facts that are the same whether you are pottering around a tiny park in a big city with your toy poodle or running across the wild moors with your pack of muddy spaniels.

Before getting into the details of walking your dog, it's worth giving some consideration to the question 'why do dogs want to go for walks?' It might seem as though the answer is obvious – 'because they enjoy them' – but we need to do better than that if we're really going to understand what motivates our dogs, and therefore make sure we all get the most out of this time together.

When I thought about this question between consultations at the surgery, the answer didn't seem immediately obvious – but then, as I thought about what drove me in my everyday life, one solution to the mystery seemed blindingly obvious – dogs like to exercise because exercise is work to a dog and we all have that innate work ethic that stems from our distant evolutionary past. Now this theory will take a little clarification and it's not an idea that's recognised by the animal behaviour world at large as far as I'm aware, so I am out on a limb somewhat. Having said that, I do believe there is something in what I'm thinking so bear with me!

In their wild existence, the purpose of exercise is to bring the reward of food through hunting and scavenging, and to defend the pack against rivals and predators through territorial patrols. Both of these are functions that are absolutely fundamental to the survival of these wild dogs, and are likely to be hardwired into their consciousness at a very deep level. Modern dogs, therefore, are highly likely to retain the basic instinct that tells them that exercise is both rewarding and necessary – and this explains, at least to a certain degree, the innate enthusiasm for our modern domestic dogs to get out and about on a walk. The urge to head out 'on patrol' with the pack leader is the equivalent of our inbuilt feeling that we need to spend our lives in a constructive manner, whether it be working for a living or raising children. Our desires are more complex than those of dogs, but the basic theory holds that both species have a deep, evolutionary need to be active and productive – as, without this, neither species would have survived the long and brutal evolutionary road to our current positions.

So I believe that part of our dogs' desire to go for a walk is down to their ancestors' association between exercise and rewarding productivity, an association that is still burning deep inside the minds of our modern dogs. But that is not the whole story by a long way. Dogs have other motivators that get them bouncing off the walls when you put your shoes on and bring out their lead, and these include the control of a territory, and the simple emotion of fun which I suspect is probably more important than many would give credit to.

Before we get on to the emotional side of dog walking, I would like to consider territory for a minute. There's no doubt that dogs are territorial animals but not to the same degree as pure carnivores such as cats for example, whose entire lives are dominated by the establishment and defence of a territory. Dogs' territories are looser and less well defined than those of cats, but they still exist, and that is why male dogs in particular like to spend their walks urine marking as they go. This basic habit is a clear act of territorial behaviour and demonstrates how important territory is even to our domesticated modern dogs. Other actions that dogs take on walks that are related to territorial behaviour include defecation, as faeces are just as potent a territorial marker as urine thanks to the intense scents imparted on the faecal matter by the dog's anal glands, and interactions with other dogs they meet – the classic bottom-smelling routine. So there is no doubt that territorial behavioural instincts are another important driver that gets your dog out of the door and wagging his tail at the gate ready for his walk.

Fun is a contentious issue when it comes to dogs – many people would question whether such a seemingly uniquely human emotion can have any place in canine behaviour – but

I think it's obvious that domestic dogs have fun and having fun motivates them. And the answer to the question of why fun is such an important emotion for our dogs, when it probably plays a far less important role in the lives of non-domestic animals including our dogs' ancestors, lies in my view that the single biggest difference between the average domestic dog and the average wild dog is neutering. When we remove the sex hormones from our pets in their adolescence, we effectively freeze certain aspects of their character development at this time. Without testosterone and oestrogen coursing through their veins, our pet dogs do not undergo many of the psychological changes that adulthood usually brings. The diminishing of the sense of fun is one of those changes. Just think about how our human children differ in terms of their enjoyment and motivation by fun and compare it to how that emotion motivates adults – it's still there, but in a less pronounced form. It's the same with dogs – puppies are naturally driven by a sense of fun which is an essential tool in the learning process, encouraging them to explore and experiment with their environment and litter mates, but this is lost to a large degree when the serious issues of adulthood arise. Neutering stops this change in its tracks and leaves our emasculated adult dogs with a puppyish sense of fun and enjoyment that sets them apart from their un-neutered or un-spayed compatriots.

My hypothesis is that one of the effects – and I believe it's a positive one – of neutering our dogs is that it allows them to retain their sense of fun from puppyhood, and this then becomes an important motivator when it comes to exercise and walks.

Before moving on to look at how, when and where you walk your dog, if we are going to be complete in our picture of the motivations behind dog walking, it's worth also thinking about our own reasons for wanting to walk the dog, as they are just as important in many ways as those of the dog. Again there's an obvious answer – 'because the dog wants to go' – but if that's the only answer then the implication is that dog ownership is a one-way relationship, with the dog benefiting from our altruistic behaviours, which doesn't make sense to me. Of course, responding to the desires of your dog is an important factor and walking a dog in the pouring rain when it's clear that it's only the dog that wants to go for the walk is part of our responsibility as a dog owner. But, thinking in more general terms, there must be motivations that drive us to want to walk the dog beyond simply responding to his needs. And I think one answer to this question is rooted deep in human psychology, which is a subject I have almost complete ignorance of, so you will have to excuse me if I lapse into unscientific language at this point to get my idea across. I suspect that there is something inherent in the act of leaving the home and wandering the countryside that gives us pleasure. I'm not sure why or how this works, but I do know that the simple act of spending time without human company and beyond the boundaries of your normal life, whether it be family or work, can have an immensely positive effect on your state of mind, and that's a reward that surely drives, at least to some extent, our desire to take the dog for a walk. I know personally there is something special about that time I get to escape the pressures of work and the hustle and bustle of family life to just walk and think. Sharing that experience with another person would change it completely – not necessarily in a bad way, but it would lose that peace that allows for contemplation and introspection – but in so many ways a dog is the ideal companion with which to share this kind of experience. A dog provides a focus and reason for the walk, he provides companionship without being intrusive, and he provides distraction and stimulus to help creative thought processes flourish.

So, for me, the number-one motivator that gets me out walking Jack, above and beyond my feeling of responsibility towards him, is to give myself that escape from everyday life and allow myself the luxury of time to think and to relax. Naturally, before we leave this subject it's important to mention some of the other reasons that undoubtedly play their part – the desire to keep fit, meet friends, socialise and so on – but for me they all play second fiddle to our basic need to feed our soul on the pure escapism a dog walk provides.

MORE THAN JUST A WALK IN THE PARK – HEARING DOGS IN ACTION
One of my favourite charities is Hearing Dogs for Deaf People. This fantastic organisation trains dogs to help people with hearing difficulties cope with their everyday lives by alerting them to sounds and dangers they might otherwise miss. For example, trained Hearing Dogs will tell their owners when there is someone at the door, or if the phone rings or the

smoke alarm sounds – all noises which those of us lucky enough to have good hearing take for granted but which could have a major impact on your life if you were unable to hear.

However, alerting owners to sounds is only one part of the role of a Hearing Dog and after talking to many recipients of these wonderful dogs I can see that in fact there is a much greater advantage that they bring to their human companions – the benefits that come from taking a dog for a walk. It's so easy for a person with hearing problems to become isolated and even housebound as their social confidence diminishes, and the simple act of being forced to get out and walk their Hearing Dog twice a day can have an amazing effect on their lives.

'I used to stay at home all day and never go out unless I had to,' one Hearing Dog recipient told me, 'and I ended up being so isolated I became depressed. But then, when Sammy arrived and I had to take him out for his walks, I found that I was gradually getting more and more confident – people I met saw his Hearing Dogs jacket so they knew straight away my hearing wasn't good, and that gave me much more confidence to talk to people. Now I'm out and about all the time, and it's fair to say Sammy really has changed my life!'

So walking a dog can have benefits far beyond the obvious, and in some cases transform people's lives.

Having explored the human and canine case for dog walks, it's time to think in more detail about the practical aspects of a dog walk and how different types of dog walks can play different roles in your ever-evolving relationship with your dog.

At its most simple level, a dog walk involves the owner

taking the dog out to an open space and exercising them for a period of time before returning home. But given the long list of motivations that drive our dog walks, it is rarely that simple – there is always a sub-plot to any dog walk, from your dog's desire to check his territory for intruders, to your wish to contemplate problems at work by yourself. So to make things easier, I think it's worth looking at different kinds of dog walks and thinking about how they can be used to best effect for the benefit of you and your dog.

There are probably a thousand ways to classify dog walks, but here is my attempt to define five different types of dog walks and their key features:

1. Routine. This is the everyday walk focused primarily around your dog's needs rather than your own. It is the everyday walk that Mr Smith and Rover take each morning to allow Rover to empty his bowels and sniff his way around his territory.

2. Functional. As the name suggests, this is a walk with a purpose. This purpose could be fetching the paper from the shop or picking up the kids from school, but, whatever it is, it is not a walk for walking's sake.

3. Recreational. These tend to be longer walks that are based more on your own motivations than your dog's. Recreational walks often also involve the whole family and possibly friends as well, and are less structured, more relaxed and more complete experiences than functional walks.

4. Educational. Walks as part of a training purpose can be

thought of as educational and generally have quite a different character to recreational or routine walks.

5. Pure pleasure. These are walks with one purpose and one purpose only – to have fun!

Firstly, let's consider the routine walk. This is probably the most important category as it's the kind of walk that you and your dog are going to share day in day out for many years. Although routine by nature, these walks are not dull, particularly from the dog's point of view, and in fact are probably best considered by using our work analogy again; routine walks are your dog's day job, getting out in his territory with the pack leader, inspecting a well-known route and reinforcing his territorial markings as he goes. It's crucial stuff and therefore your dog is likely to feel stressed if for any reason he is denied this regular outing – imagine how frustrated you'd feel if you were forced to miss an important regular meeting at work – so it is important to keep these routine walks regular and predictable to reduce this kind of distress.

Routine walks themselves vary enormously in their length and character. For some dogs, a quick five minutes around the park is all they get of a morning, but, for others, their regular walk consists of an hour or more of strenuous exercise following their super-fit owner. The main thing to consider when looking at the suitability of your regular walks for your dog is how it suits their temperament and physical character. As routine walks make up a significant proportion of a dog's weekly exercise, it's important that they provide sufficient exercise to satisfy the dog in question – so a manic Springer Spaniel or Border Collie will benefit from a much longer and more rigorous routine walk schedule than a smaller or older dog.

As well as the length and type of walk, it is worth thinking about where you walk your dog on these routine walks. Often you'll have little or no choice – it's the park or nothing – but if you do have a choice then consider opting for somewhere that is not too popular with other dogs, to give your dog the chance to establish at least some sense of territory of his own. If his routine walks are all in crowded parks with hundreds of other dogs to distract and compete with him, he will miss out on the ability to mark out and maintain his own patch of the world, which I think is important to most dogs. Obviously this is not going to be possible for many dog owners, but it's something to consider if you do have the luxury of choice. It's also worth trying to stick to just a couple of routine routes, again to give your dog the chance to establish himself territorially and also to allow him to get into a routine. Dogs are creatures of habit and constantly varying their routine walks may be appealing for you but it is likely to be less appreciated by your dog.

Functional walks by contrast are much less to do with the desires of your dog and all to do with a necessity of your life, whether it be an errand to the shop, or perhaps something less obvious such as a training run for an athlete. Whatever the function of the walk, you just need to give some consideration to its suitability for your dog – clearly you shouldn't subject an elderly King Charles Spaniel with a heart problem to a five-mile training run in the hot sun for example – but there might also be less obvious issues to consider such as whether the route of your walk takes you near busy roads or, if your dog is nervous around other dogs, in busy parks. Due to their very nature as functional exercises, there is usually little flexibility and room to consider what your dog is going to get out of the walk, but that's fine as long as an unsuitable functional walk doesn't become an unsuitable routine walk.

Recreational walks are one of the great pleasures of dog ownership – that excuse to take the family out on a ramble through the woods, or perhaps it's just you and the dog spending some quality time together chasing sticks and exploring the countryside. Whatever the reason, a recreational walk is the ultimate expression of your relationship with your dog. The key to a successful recreational walk is the blending of your motivations with your dog's so that everyone comes home satisfied and happy. We've already identified the key walk motivators of a dog – work ethic, territory and fun – and the likely motivators of the owner – leaving the home for the good of the soul, exercise, socialisation and so on – so getting a recreational walk right is simply about considering all of those motivations and making sure as many as possible can be satisfied.

Therefore, from the dog's point of view, a good recreational walk needs to consist of a decent amount of exercise to satisfy his work ethic, the ability to tend to his territory and the opportunity for some good clean fun. Fom your point of view, it should deliver that soul-enhancing outdoor break from the modern world, along with opportunities for socialisation and exercise. It's not always possible to combine every element in one walk. If your recreational walk takes you to a new location, for instance, then your dog is going to be unable to tend to his home territory, but, if you make sure he's busy having fun and getting plenty of exercise, then this isn't necessarily something to worry about.

An example of a successful recreational walk would be one that the Smiths take with their friends the Jones at the weekend. The families meet at a local woodland park and head off for a couple of hours strolling through the woods, Rover and Fido chasing each other in and out of trees, stopping only to cock their legs intermittently. The families socialise, the children play with each other and the dogs, and the whole affair ends up at a cafe where the people undo all the good work of the exercise with a bun and a cup of tea, and the dogs drain bowls of refreshing water and hunt for tit-bits among the cafe tables. By the time the families return home, everyone is happy, dogs included, with motivations satisfied across the board.

Before we finish with recreational walks, I want to bring up yet another contentious subject that really divides dog owners – and vets for that matter – and it's the issue of throwing sticks for dogs. The accepted wisdom of the veterinary community is that throwing sticks for dogs is a bad and irresponsible activity as every year dogs are injured, and, in extremely rare cases, killed, by accidents involving sticks. The main way these accidents occur is when sticks are thrown and end up stuck in the ground with a sharp end pointing upwards when they land. The dog, rushing to fetch the stick, can't stop in time to react to the stick's position and ends up impaling himself on the stick. The injuries caused by such an accident can be horrendous and are often life-threatening as the sticks usually impale the head and neck, leaving deep wounds impregnated with dirt. Most vets have had to deal with these kinds of injuries during their career, so it's not surprising that the general view within the profession is that throwing sticks is too dangerous to be acceptable.

But – and I think it's a big but – you have to look at the big picture and assess the risk rationally rather than jumping to the conclusion that a behaviour is unacceptable simply because it can cause injury. Given the number of sticks that are thrown for dogs on walks every year, the number of injuries is incredibly low. I wouldn't attempt to put a figure on it, and I doubt if anyone could produce an accurate quantitative estimate of the actual risk, but I'm sure the risk is far lower than most perceive it to be – and certainly far lower than the risk of other injuries such as road-traffic accidents, ruptured cruciate ligaments from chasing balls and fight wounds from other dogs, to name but three. The problem is that the injuries tend to be severe and memorable to both vets and owners and tend to exaggerate the scale of the problem in people's minds – it's very hard to be objective when you've just treated a dog with a stick stuck in their throat. But objectivity is essential if we are going to make the blanket recommendation of 'no one should throw a stick for their dog' because there are negative impacts to making that recommendation. After all, dogs love chasing things and, despite the availability of alternatives such as balls and toys, there are many occasions when a dog owner finds themselves on a walk with nothing but a stick to hand.

If you intend to adhere to the recommendation, such occasions would be less enjoyable for dog and owner than they otherwise could be, which is why I don't agree with the recommendation, and in fact why I continue to throw a stick for Jack every day. Life is for living and, if we eliminate every risk, there is nothing left but boredom!

Having said that, I do believe we have a responsibility to minimise the risk any activity poses to our dogs if there is a way that can be achieved without completely sacrificing the benefits it brings. And, with stick throwing, there are clear ways in which you can take steps to keep the risks to a minimum and allow your dog to enjoy this centuries-old activity as safely as possible. Here are my top tips for safe stick throwing:

- Choose your stick well – long or short sticks are better than mid-length sticks which are more likely to end up at the right height to impale if they get stuck in the ground, so aim for either a stick that is shorter than the distance from your dog's tummy to the ground, or longer than his total height. Sticks should also be as blunt ended as possible, and ideally not be straight – a blunt, curved stick is very unlikely to end up causing injury.
- Aim well – try to make sure your stick lands well in advance of your dog arriving at it, so you give your dog plenty of time to see the stick land and approach it accordingly. So throw the stick to one side of your dog's expected trajectory and throw it far enough to give him time to adjust before he reaches it.

- Throw well – it's better to throw a stick with a side-arm action so it rotates horizontally in the air rather than vertically, which would give it much more chance of sticking into the ground, so forget your cricket bowling technique and go for an agricultural side-arm fling!
- Keep vigilant – a few minutes of heavy-duty dog chewing can change a stick from long and blunt to short and sharp, so keep an eye on the stick and change it for a fresh one if it becomes dangerous.

Educational walks are the next category to consider and these are walks with a definite purpose which fit into a training regime. It could be that your goal is to perfect your dog's recall skills or obedience on the lead, or perhaps you're out and about with the aim of socialising your dog to stimuli such as meeting other dogs or walking near busy roads. Whatever the plan, an educational walk needs some thought if it is going to achieve its aims – and, importantly, not have any undesirable negative effects. For example, a walk designed to habituate your dog to meeting other dogs while on the lead to improve his manners and behaviour could backfire if your walk takes you past a particularly aggressive dog who launches at your dog in an intimidating frenzy and scares the living daylights out of him. Or a walk designed to work on recall training that takes you to a busy park full of distractions is far less likely to be a success than if you'd chosen a quieter location. So make sure you think about the aims of your educational walk and tailor your route and itinerary to suit.

Last, and by no means least, is my category of pure pleasure walks, and these are simply walks for walks' sake. I guess in reality there's not much difference between a recreational walk and a pure pleasure walk, but in my mind there is something unique about a walk which is usually just you and the dog, which has no purpose other than to enjoy each other's company and the sights, smells and views of the great outdoors. These walks are often spur-of-the-moment events, with little or no planning, where you (or sometimes the dog!) decide that there's nothing you'd rather do than get out of the house and head to the park or up into the hills for half an hour and get some fresh air. Personally my pure pleasure walks usually happen in the evening when, fed up with watching rubbish on the TV, I suddenly decide to get up, grab Jack's lead and head out for a walk. I'm often only out for twenty minutes or so, but the spontaneity of the walk and the feeling of freedom that such a sudden decision brings really fills me with exhilaration and I come back refreshed and rewarded. Jack also loves these spur-of-the-moment excursions as they're an unexpected bonus in an otherwise often routine day, and I can tell how much he shares my pleasure in these outings.

So, with walks analysed and categorised, there's only one more topic to discuss before we move on to thinking about family time, and that's how long and how far to walk your dog. The classic answer to this question is that all dogs, regardless of their size, age or character, need two good walks every day. While I agree with the basic premise that all dogs need regular exercise, I don't think it's right to generalise in this way, and that the right answer for one dog may not be the same right answer for another dog. As I've mentioned previously, I think it's crucial that we always remember that dogs are individuals and treat them as such if we are going to build successful relationships with them. If we resort to living by generalisations such as 'two walks a day come rain or shine', then we are not treating our canine companions with the respect and understanding that they deserve. By thinking about our own dog and our own lives, we can each come up with an answer that is relevant and appropriate rather than relying on a blanket generalisation.

For example, let's go back to the Smiths and Rover the Labrador. Mr Smith walks Rover twice a day because that's what he's always done and that's what's expected of a caring dog owner. And for Rover this arrangement works very well, and, although he'd like more walks each day, he's content with two and they keep him physically and mentally fit and happy.

Mr Smith's friend Mrs Davis also has a Labrador, but she's an old girl called Mavis and over the last few year's she's been struggling with her hips, causing her pain and discomfort, particularly after long walks. Mrs Davis, however, is sticking to her usual routine of two walks a day, come rain or shine, and Mavis valiantly tries to keep up and do her canine duty. In reality, though, Mavis would prefer a few hours' pottering around the garden to two long walks each day, as this would ease the strain on her joints while still giving her the stimulation and enjoyment of getting outside and sniffing around her patch.

From these two examples, it's easy to see how a 'one size fits all' recommendation of two walks a day is not going to be appropriate for all dogs and all families. So, if you're not going to use this general rule, how do you work out what's right for your dog?

This is really where you have to use your own judgement and listen to what your dog is trying to tell you. A young and active dog full of energy and enthusiasm will make his desire for many long walks every day blatantly obvious to you, but picking up on the more subtle signals from a less active dog, such as Mavis, is not always as straightforward. In these instances, there is a case for taking advice and your vet is the best person to help you decide what's appropriate for your dog. Particularly for older dogs, a thorough physical check-over is important, and will enable your vet to give you specific and relevant advice about a suitable exercise regime that will help keep your dog both physically healthy and happy.

Obviously, any regime you decide is ideal for your dog also has to work for you and your family – living with your dog is all about a partnership and it won't work if it's too one-sided – so don't forget to take into account the amount of time you have available and how much exercise you enjoy when coming up with your own answer to the 'how many walks a day' question.

Joe's TV Casebook

A QUESTION OF EXERCISE

On my regular vet spot on *The Wright Stuff* on Five, I hold an open surgery where viewers can call in with questions to put to me about their pets. It's live, and I often have no idea what questions are coming, so it can be quite stressful as I have to come up with helpful answers to all sorts of questions on the spur of the moment. Many of the questions are relatively easy to answer, but occasionally I get something that really makes me think – and a few months ago I had a deceptively simple question that really started me thinking about the issue of how often to walk a dog.

The question came from a viewer called Pauline, and she asked me whether she really needed to take her little Shi Tzu for a walk at all, as he didn't enjoy them one bit. She had been repeatedly told that all dogs needed two walks every day.

I was about to answer that yes, she really should be taking the dog out twice day, because that's the accepted answer and the one that came naturally to mind. But before I opened my mouth I thought about it for a second and, when I did reply, my answer was very different to my initial thought.

'No, I don't think you should take him for a walk if he doesn't enjoy it,' I said, surprising myself with what I was saying, 'as long as he's getting exercise in and around the home, and he's not putting on weight, there's no reason to drag him along on a walk he's not going to enjoy just for the sake of it.'

Pauline was very relieved by my answer – but Matthew Wright, the show's host, asked me about it after the end of the phone-in session as he couldn't believe that a vet was recommending not walking a dog. I stood by my view and explained that dogs are individuals and you have to do what's best for each dog based on their own needs. I'm not sure I entirely convinced him – but the more I've thought about it since, the more I'm sure I've got a good point!

FAMILY TIME

For most pet dog owners, their dog is one of the family, and the majority of the time of the dog's day is spent interacting with the family. This family time makes up a large proportion of many dogs' lives, and so it's vital to get the basics of this time together right if you're to have a fulfilling relationship with your dog.

When the dog is interacting with the family – and family could mean anything from you on your own to a nuclear family with children and grandparents depending on your circumstances – he's really interacting with the other members of his pack, and this important fact needs to be at the back of your mind whenever you're thinking about issues or challenges that may have arisen. Like all other aspects of living with your dog, it's important to think about all situations from your dog's perspective as well as your own as this is the only way you'll ever get close to understanding why your dog acts the way he does, and therefore the only way you'll ever hope to change his behaviour if he's not doing as he should.

Family time is all about everyday interactions and situations – mealtimes, busy family play time with children racing about the house, quiet evening relaxation in front of the TV, mowing the lawn and so on. It's important that your dog has a clear role in these situations, a role that he – and you – understand, because ambiguity is not something dogs are really programmed to deal with. Dogs live in a remarkably black and white world when it comes to rules, and it's important to help your dog feel comfortable with any given situation by setting out clearly the ground rules that you expect to apply.

To give this theory some practical relevance, here are some examples of how various situations might be perceived differently by you and your dog – and how some simple steps can overcome any potential confusion and ensure harmonious family time for all.

MEALTIMES

You think... this is a time for you and your (human) family to eat, and spend quality time together, but the dog is a pain as he's always getting under our feet, begging for food and we often have to shut him away.

The dog thinks... food, glorious food – but why aren't I getting any? What have I done wrong? Perhaps if I try that begging behaviour I'll get rewarded with some, after all it worked last time! Oh no, what's this, I've been sent to my bed for begging, when last time I got food – what on earth's going on?!

The issue in this example is inconsistency in the owner's response to the dog at mealtimes. Begging behaviour is sometimes rewarded with food, and sometimes it's punished.

There is also confusion over the dog's role at the mealtime – is he expected to join in, or just watch, or spend the time shut away in another room?

To avoid problems like this, there's a need to firmly establish in your dog's mind the idea that human mealtimes and dog mealtimes are different events and there is no crossover between the two. Once it's clear that human food in the context of a human meal (ie on a plate on the table) is not for dogs under any circumstances, your dog will understand and not try to beg for food (provided you never give in!). If you do want to give your dog leftovers, then saving them after your meal and giving them to him in his own dish at his dinnertime is a much better approach than allowing him to effectively join in your mealtimes by begging and receiving scraps and leftovers from the table. To further enforce this point that the canine and human members of the family pack have different mealtimes, make sure you don't eat while your dog is eating his dinner – respect his dinner in the same way you expect him to respect yours.

PLAY TIME

You think… a time for the whole family to have fun – children racing around, and the dog joining in all the fun, wagging his tail and chasing balls in the garden.

The dog thinks… this is great, loads of attention and excitement, I'll bark to let everyone know how happy I am, and then jump up and down in excitement!

This is a fairly harmonious example, in which the dog's role as centre of attention and chief entertainer is clearly established and interaction between all members of the family is on a level playing field with the normal pack hierarchy partially suspended in all the excitement.

This is all very well, but this kind of situation where the usual rules of etiquette that govern your dog's behaviour are temporarily suspended does allow for things to get out of hand – and potentially risk damaging your relationship with your dog. Problems can arise either accidentally, if the dog gets a little over-exuberant, or more seriously if your dog takes the opportunity of the relaxed nature of the situation to try to exert a degree of dominance. Therefore, it's essential that you keep gently reminding your dog that, while play time might mean he can get away with behaviour that would normally be unacceptable, there has been no material change in the hierarchy of the family pack and he's still at the bottom of the social order. Simple things such as your making the decision to end games and take toys away with you rather than allowing your dog to dictate terms, and winning any competitive games such as tug of war, are all that's usually required.

This approach is particularly important for children, as dogs with ambitions to climb the social ladder will be likely to target those lowest down in the order, and that is usually the children. So, if you spot any sign of your dog trying to exert dominance over you or especially your children, make sure you take steps to reiterate the social order and make it clear that there is no scope for upward social mobility in your family pack!

RELAXATION TIME

Your think… ah, at last the children are in bed, I can put the TV on and put my feet up. The dog's had his walk so I can leave him to snooze in the corner.

Your dog thinks… it's nice and calm, I feel safe and relaxed, time for a snooze… but hold on a minute, what was that sound, I better jump up and bark to alert the family to the danger!

After a busy day most families like to wind down and relax in the evening, and, for most family dogs, this quiet time represents a chance to catch up on some napping and generally enjoy the peace and quiet of the evening. However, not all dogs 'do' relaxation as well as others, and for some an hour or two of inactivity can be more stressful than the active times in the day, particularly for energetic or intelligent dogs, and in other cases there may be other factors that make it hard for your dog to join in and relax alongside the rest of the family. These factors could include external stimuli such as noises or smells that you're blissfully unaware of, or mental stimuli such as conditioned expectations of events later on such as a late-evening walk or snack, and are often the underlying cause of agitation or restlessness for dogs during these supposedly quiet times.

Relaxation time is not just about putting your feet up and letting the dog snooze in his bed, it can also be a great opportunity to bond with your dog and spend quality time together. Simple things like sitting on the floor and giving the dog a cuddle, or grooming him as you watch TV will all help to build positive associations in your dog's mind, the basis of building a strong relationship with him. So just remember, next time you're bored watching TV and the dog's equally bored watching you watch the TV, why not turn off the telly and spend some time with your dog – it can be surprisingly rewarding for you as much as for your dog. Sometimes we tend to take our dogs for granted and slip into a routine of life that has little time in it for affection and simple but positive interactions, and we need to force ourselves out of this pattern and make time for our relationship with our dogs, in the same way that we need to do this with the rest of our family and friends. Somehow it's easier to forget the dog and put him at the bottom of our priority list – but never forget how important you are to your dog and how wonderful it is for him to have your undivided loving attention, even if it's only for a short period every day. Little moments like ten minutes spent scratching an ear or rubbing a tummy can be amazingly important and in the long term can be crucial to your relationship with your dog.

Joe's Pets

AN EVENING WITH JACK

Being half Spaniel and half Collie, Jack is a clever boy, and also full of energy, which makes it all the more surprising that he likes nothing more than retiring to his bed in the corner of the living room once the children are in bed to doze contentedly for several hours.

However, as soon as it gets to within an hour or so of

bedtime, he starts to become more and more alert, and jumps up excitedly whenever I move or stand up from the sofa. He looks up at me in expectation, knowing that his late-evening stroll and bedtime snack are not too far away. While this can be quite endearing, it can also get quite wearing as having Jack on tenterhooks waiting to go out makes it hard to relax and can rather spoil the air of calm and peace that my wife and I are usually enjoying at this time of the evening.

This means that I often end up doing exactly the wrong thing and giving in to Jack's expectant excitement just to get some peace – so he gets rewarded for his excitable behaviour with his walk and treat, and I finally get some peace and quiet! I know that this is the wrong approach as by giving in to his behaviour I am effectively using inadvertent operant conditioning to teach Jack that a behaviour pattern that I find annoying is one that is rewarded and therefore encouraged.

Knowing that something is wrong and doing the right thing about it are two very different things, though. Thinking logically, I should be more disciplined and not give in to Jack's demands, and only take him out at the set time that I decide, but putting this theory into practice at the end of a long day when the easy option is to give in is easier said than done!

STRESSFUL SITUATIONS

You think… I'll just run the vacuum cleaner round.

Your dog thinks… Oh my God, what's that terrible monster following my owner around the living room making that howling sound – should I attack it? Should I bark? I know, I'll run away and squeeze myself into a corner and put my paws over my ears until it stops!

However hard we try to socialise our dogs to all the sights and sounds of the modern human world, there will always be some situations that dogs find stressful, and it's important to help them to cope as best we can. Obviously and as discussed earlier on, prevention is the best approach and socialising your dog to experiences such as vacuum cleaners and lawn mowers while they are young enough to learn that these are not threatening monsters is ideal. However, socialisation is not 100 per cent effective even if done properly (which it often isn't), and little factors that you or I might think insignificant such as differences between the sound and appearance of two different vacuum cleaners can be surprisingly important to your dog. For example, he might take the sound of a Dyson in his stride but be completely freaked out by a Hoover, simply because of subtle differences in their characteristics.

So, while socialisation is clearly well worth undertaking, there will always be situations that arise in family life that upset your dog and you need to know how to cope with these in order to minimise the stress your dog suffers and any negative behaviours that might occur as a result.

To illustrate this point, let's consider a classic example where the dog is terrified of the vacuum cleaner and disappears as soon as it comes out of the cupboard to hide as far away as possible, often ending up so scared he shivers, shakes and wets himself. This example may sound extreme but it's not at all uncommon and I wouldn't be surprised if most of you reading this either have a dog who reacts like this to some stimulus or other, or know someone who has a dog who does.

So what can you do about this as it's obviously causing the dog distress and you inconvenience when he wets the carpet? Well, one solution that some people would try is to punish the dog for wetting the floor, and I hope you can see that this is not a suitable approach to consider as the dog is not voluntarily making a mess and is only doing so in response to extreme fear. Punishing him will serve only to reinforce this fear and make matters worse.

A much more positive and successful strategy is to try to gradually replace the negative associations your dog has with the stimulus of the vacuum cleaner with positive ones, with the goal of ultimately making him see the appearance of the vacuum cleaner as a positive event rather than a negative one. It may be impossible to go this far with some very timid dogs, but you should at the very least be able to reduce fear levels sufficiently to make the problem much less acute and more manageable. The way to do this is through the simple technique of classical conditioning – changing the subconscious link between the sight and sound of the machine from one of fear and loathing to one of positive reward. Start gradually by getting the vacuum cleaner out but not turning it on, and, while it is sitting in the corner of the room, spend some positive time playing and rewarding your dog using his favourite treats. You will need to spend some time repeating this (remember the three 'R's of training) until you get to the stage where the sight of the vacuum cleaner no longer causes your dog stress but instead makes him excited because of the link to a treat or other reward such as attention from you.

Once you've created this positive association with the silent machine, it's time to move to the next stage and turn it on. Try to do this at as low a level as possible to begin with, and it's important that you show no sign of stress or anxiety at this stage. It's all too easy for you to be tense when anticipating the reaction your dog will have, and this simply serves to reinforce your dog's view that there must be something to be scared of. So turn it on with a happy smile and, if your dog shows signs of fear or stress, ignore him and move on with the positive rewarding activity as if nothing has happened. The worst thing you can do is make a big fuss if your dog does react badly, so try to keep calm and act as if there's absolutely nothing to worry about – and your dog will pick up on this and feel reassured rather than stressed.

With some persistence you should be able to cure your dog of any negative reactions to stimuli such as vacuum cleaners or lawn mowers using this technique, which is also known as desensitisation.

WORKING WITH YOUR DOG

In this final part of the chapter on living with your dog I'm going to take a brief look at how our dogs can become more than just companions – they can become work colleagues as well, often taking on invaluable roles in our working lives. People are often surprised by the aptitude that our dogs show for working roles and their diverse talents for activities such as rounding up sheep or helping blind people navigate the streets, but, if you think back over the history of the domestication process, we have spent the last 10,000 years or more artificially selecting for these exact traits. It's only been much more recently that dogs have been considered companions rather than workers, and so it's more logical really to wonder at how our canine companions have become such good pets rather than such good workers.

Working dogs perform a vast range of tasks from search and rescue to sniffing out cancer cells, but underlying all of these roles are two basic building blocks – obedience and innate skill. The obedience side of the equation has come from millennia of domestication through selective breeding reinforced by suitable training regimes. The skills our dogs bring to their working roles, such as their acute sense of smell and instinctive herding behaviours, are much older traits which have been shaped not by man but by countless years of evolution through natural selection. The art of the human 'master' in working situations is to help the dog to use these innate skills in a relevant way, a combination of human and canine skills at the heart of all successful working-dog relationships.

Much of my experience with working dogs has come through a personal relationship with a very special charity called Hearing Dogs for Deaf People. I first started working with them four years ago, when I rowed a giant dog bowl down the river Thames to raise money to support them, and, since that first rather eccentric collaboration, we've worked closely together on several further fundraising projects. I have also seen firsthand the amazing work of the dogs they train, and how crucial this is for the recipients who benefit from their lifelong assistance. So I thought, rather than talk in general terms about working dogs, I would instead focus on the work of Hearing Dogs.

The idea of training Hearing Dogs to assist deaf people was first introduced to the UK in 1982 after Lady Beatrice Wright and vet Bruce Fogle saw a similar scheme in America. The first dog selected for training, Favour, a tan and white crossbred dog, was selected from a rescue centre and Hearing Dogs was launched at Crufts that year.

The charity still takes a number of puppies and young dogs from rescue centres and dog wardens, and has a member of staff in the Republic of Ireland keeping an eye out for stray and abandoned dogs that might be suitable for the work. Dogs are also donated to Hearing Dogs by breeders and members of the public whose circumstances may have changed which means the animals can no longer be kept as pets. Compared to dogs bred specifically to become Hearing Dogs, these dogs generally need a little bit longer to settle down during the early socialisation period, but most of them go on to make fantastic Hearing Dogs, thus not only gaining an improvement in their own fortunes but also dramatically improving the lives of the deaf people they assist. The charity also has a breeding scheme which helps to ensure a steady flow of puppies coming through the system.

Since the young dogs come from a variety of sources, there is a variety of breeds and crossbreeds. The wonderful thing about Hearing Dogs is that there is no such thing as a typical Hearing Dog – as long as the temperament is right, size and breed does not really matter. This is one of the things that really appealed to me when I first visited one of their centres, and also made me realise that any breed of dog has the potential to become a working dog, not just the usual suspects such as Labradors or Golden Retrievers.

Having said that, there are quite specific requirements for the individual dogs who go on to become Hearing Dogs. They need to be friendly and biddable, and have an intelligence and responsiveness to sounds which will ensure they will work off their own initiative once they are placed with a deaf person. So, when a dog has been offered to the charity, he is assessed thoroughly to make sure he possesses the right qualities and the temperament to cope with all the training he will undergo before being placed with a deaf owner.

When a dog has been assessed and identified as having the right characteristics, he will then live with one of the charity's many volunteer puppy socialisers. These wonderful people are prepared to take a young, non-housetrained puppy into their homes for up to a year, and spend a great deal of time and love teaching the youngster basic manners and obedience. Handlers will housetrain the pups, take them into busy environments, introduce them to all sorts of people and experiences to ensure they are fully socialised, as well as teaching them the basic training skills of sitting quietly, coming back when called and staying in one place when told.

It is during this socialising stage that some dogs will show characteristics that are not suitable for a future hearing dog, and they will be withdrawn from the scheme. As registered assistance dogs, hearing dogs are required to reach a very high standard of obedience, training and behaviour as they will be allowed into public places where pet dogs are not. Obviously some puppies who seemed good candidates at eight weeks old may develop unacceptable traits no matter how much training they receive. Others might be too nervous or shy to cope with the very public life of a hearing dog, so it is kinder to rehome them as pet dogs. In fact, the charity actually has a waiting list of homes ready to take their so-called 'fallen angels'.

So that's how a puppy starts his hearing dog career, but what about the deaf person? How do they start the process of becoming a hearing dog recipient? Hearing Dogs for Deaf People take a great deal of care when matching a hearing dog with their prospective recipient as in many ways it is more crucial than for a regular pet dog that a perfect match is made. The applicant will be interviewed about their lifestyle, from whether they work to where they shop, in order to build up a complete picture of the type of life into which the hearing dog will fit. This is imperative when trying to find the right dog for the right person, because dogs, like people, come with different abilities and temperaments.

Once a match between dog and person has been decided, the applicant is invited to meet the dog to make sure that both parties are happy with each other. All being well, the dog will then embark on 16 weeks of advanced sound-work training, learning to become alert to the sounds specifically required by their recipient. These sounds typically include the telephone, doorbell, alarm clock, cooker timer, baby cry and a call for help, as well as the danger sounds of a smoke alarm and fire bell. The dogs are trained using exactly the same positive motivational reward-based methods that we've discussed previously. Anyone witnessing a training session with these dogs will be immediately struck by the enthusiasm of the dogs and their ever-wagging tails, underlining the fact that a hearing dog's training is fun!

Upon hearing a sound, the hearing dog is trained to find his owner and touch them with a paw. The owner will ask, 'What is it?' as they will know that a sound has gone off but at this stage they will not know which one. The hearing dog will then lead his owner to the source of the sound, be it the telephone or doorbell, unless it is a danger sound, in which case he has been trained to lie down as a clear indication that there is something wrong. The onus is then on the recipient, having been told there is a danger sound, to get both themselves and their dog to a safe place.

At the end of the four months' sound-work training, the recipient is again invited to the training centre to spend a week on site with their new hearing dog, building up the bond that will strengthen over the coming years. It is during this week that the deaf person will also be trained: how to look after a hearing dog; how to continue his training at home; how to handle the dog when out and about. Most recipients say that this training week is not only incredibly exciting for them but also very tiring, as there is much for them to learn in order to maintain the high standards of training already undergone by their new canine hearing aid.

It is only at the end of the training week that recipient and hearing dog finally go home together to begin what in most cases turns out to be a very special relationship. For up to six months after the dog first goes home with his deaf owner, the partnership is still technically in training, and the charity arranges for visits to the recipient's home to check that the relationship is all that it should be, and to iron out any teething problems that may occur in those early days.

If all is well, and the relationship is strong between dog and owner, an assessor from the charity will visit to put the hearing dog through his paces for his final partnership qualification. This will include checking his sound-work, making sure he is happy being handled, watching his behaviour when out and about in public places as well as maintaining obedience. These are the standards set down for all assistance dogs because they are allowed access to places where pet dogs are not, and as such they must be above reproach in behaviour, obedience and hygiene. If the hearing dog passes all these hurdles, he will become a fully qualified hearing dog and receive a burgundy Hearing Dog jacket which he will wear at all times when out in public.

Hearing dogs dramatically and completely change the lives of their deaf owners. Deafness is an invisible disability, and one that is not generally well tolerated by the public.

Many deaf people suffer isolation, loneliness and depression, and recipients of hearing dogs very often say that their isolation prior to receiving their dog made them even contemplate suicide. The obvious practical work that a hearing dog offers can be understood by most people: for example, being alerted to an alarm clock means no more missed appointments; and the security of being told about danger sounds when out in public and in the home cannot be underestimated. However, the emotional and psychological benefits are just as important. The dog's burgundy working jacket alerts the public to the owner's hearing difficulties, and also attracts people to the dog, thus encouraging social interaction for the deaf person. Social inclusion is the inalienable right of every human being, and, for deaf people, a hearing dog provides that and so much more.

WORKING DOGS: HEARING DOGS IN ACTION

Thelma is an attractive mongrel who was nearly three years old when Hearing Dogs selected her from Manchester Dogs' Home. Eleven months after she was selected, she was placed with her deaf owner, Chris Goard in Plymouth.

In addition to his deafness, which has increased over the years, Chris has to live with constant tinnitus (ringing in the ears) which he has found enormously stressful. He also has multiple disabilities which have resulted in his mobility being severely restricted, and he relies on the use of a wheelchair to get about. His wife, Eileen, also has health problems, suffering numerous epileptic seizures. Before Thelma, these problems meant that social life, evenings out and holidays for Chris and Eileen were completely out of the question.

However, Thelma's arrival in 2004 dramatically changed both Chris's and Eileen's lives. Being alerted to all the sounds in the home has really helped Chris, but the impact of this former rescue dog goes far beyond that, as Chris explains: 'Thelma's devotion to duty in making me aware of sounds is just great, and my confidence and quality of life is growing day by day. She has many friends in our local supermarket, and now people stop me to talk to me about her and what she can do. We have even now been on holiday to Cumbria, and are planning a big trip to a hotel for a special celebration next year: this would have been unthinkable in the past, and is all down to Thelma giving me back confidence to enjoy life again.'

It is not only the quality of Chris's life that has been vastly improved: Thelma's gentle and caring nature has made a big difference to Eileen too. Chris explains: 'Thelma has proved a life-saver when Eileen recently had a very severe seizure in the bathroom. Thelma ran to find me downstairs and alerted me. If she had not been so quick things could have been much worse, or even fatal. Earlier this year Eileen had six seizures in two days, and Thelma stayed with her all the time except to eat or tell me about sounds. Before I had Thelma, Eileen used to have a lot of seizures, up to five or six a month.

'Since Thelma has been with us, she now has fewer seizures and has even gone up to three months without one. Her consultant is convinced this is because Thelma has made life more relaxed and less stressful, and Eileen feels so much more secure when Thelma is near.'

Thelma's sensitive character, willingness to please and use of her initiative are testament to Hearing Dogs for Deaf

People's belief that rescue dogs can and do become invaluable companions and assistants for deaf people. Chris is fulsome in his praise of his beloved Thelma, and is well aware of what he and Eileen owe her: 'Having had two failed hip operations and trying to cope with deafness and caring for my wife with epilepsy, the quality of my life could not have got any worse.

'Thelma has now been part of my life for over three years and in that time has not only saved my wife's life but also tried to warn me that I was about to become unwell while having our yearly Christmas meal with our family. Not taking any notice of what Thelma was trying to tell me, she then alerted my son by pawing at his legs and would not stop until he asked, "What is it?" By that time I had the misfortune to suffer a heart condition which required urgent medical treatment within the restaurant by paramedics. She amazed everyone by her devotion to me [...] all this from a previously unwanted pet. All I can say is their loss is my gain.

'Thelma is very special to me in many ways, firstly her duty in alerting me to the sounds of the doorbell and telephone is wonderful, she enjoys doing it without question. I can now retire at night knowing she will alert me if the smoke alarm goes off and will stay and lie down until I give her a reward and cuddles.

'Believe me, to have this peace of mind at night and to put trust in your hearing dog makes a big difference to the quality of your life. She has given me the will and courage again to face the world with renewed confidence.'

Thelma won the hero dog category in the Dogs Trust Honours 2009, and her inspiring story is just one of the many examples of how the special relationship between working dogs and their recipients can transform lives.

I hope that account, for which I must thank Jenny Moir at Hearing Dogs for her help, gives you an understanding of the immensely valuable work that dogs such as hearing dogs do. Personally, I think that the relationships between working dogs such as hearing dogs and guide dogs and their human partners epitomise all that is wonderful about the way in which people and dogs can coexist so harmoniously and profitably, and there is much we can all learn as pet owners from working dogs and their lives.

FIVE

Feeding
Your Dog

In various chapters along the way we've looked at food and feeding, but in this chapter I'll spend a bit more time on the subject as I feel it's one of the most crucial aspects we need to get right if our dogs are going to live long and happy lives. A healthy diet underlies our dogs' physical health, and the way in which we feed that diet can have a significant impact on mental health and behaviour, too. If we get diet and feeding right, our dogs stand a much better chance of staying fit and healthy (and might even help to keep vets such as myself out of business!).

As we've already discussed the hows, whys and wheres of feeding in some detail, this chapter is going to focus on the practical aspects of diet and how good and bad foods can have an impact on your dog's health. But first, it's worth revisiting the basics of nutrition, as these are fundamental to everything that follows.

The main three food groups are protein, carbohydrates and fats. It's a mix of these three that makes up the vast majority of what our dogs – and ourselves – eat. In simple terms, protein is the building block of animals and is used for growth and repair; carbohydrate is fuel and is mainly converted into energy; and fat is both a fuel and carrier of essential micronutrients including fat-soluble vitamins and fatty acids. A healthy diet consists of the correct balance of these three basic groups – too much of any one type of nutrient can cause an imbalance and lead to issues such as obesity, hyperactivity or even more serious clinical diseases.

So how do we know what's the correct mix of protein, carbohydrate and fat and how do we ensure that our dogs are getting their optimal diet? Well, the good news is that, thanks to millennia of evolution in the wild, our modern dogs are very well equipped to deal with a wide range of combinations of the basic nutrients, so getting it wrong is actually harder than you might think. Out in their wild environment the ancestors of our modern domestic dogs didn't have the luxury of specially formulated diets created by scientists worrying about whether 26 per cent protein was more suitable for an active dog than 25 per cent – they simply ate what they could and their bodies adapted to make the best use of the available nutrients. While this system obviously worked, as witnessed by the survival and progress of the canine species, there is no doubt that many wild dogs lived on a diet that was far from optimal and suffered in terms of chronic health problems and relatively short life spans. Given the resources available nowadays, we can have a definite positive influence on the lives of our dogs by analysing their specific needs and feeding optimal diets that work with their naturally evolved requirements to the best effect.

As previously mentioned, there are those people who feel differently on this subject and advocate feeding dogs on a diet that replicates as closely as possible their 'ancestral diet' – primarily raw meaty bones and scavenged scraps. There is logic in this argument, as evolution has worked over many hundreds of thousands of years to perfect the canine digestive tract to suit this kind of diet, so one could therefore easily assume that a raw diet based on this evolutionary history would be the best. But there are flaws in the argument, one of the main ones being the assumption that just because a dog evolved to eat a raw diet scavenged from leftover carcasses that this is the best diet it could possibly eat. The only reason dogs ate raw scraps was because that was all there was available, hence they developed their niche role as scavengers. This does not mean that their digestive tracts have evolved in such a way that other foods might not be even better than scraps. It's a bit like saying that our eyes evolved to spot predators and find food and therefore that is the best way for us to do those things, whereas most people would agree that modern technological advances such as binoculars or cameras or computers can help us better undertake such tasks by working with our naturally evolved attributes.

I believe that, while our dogs undoubtedly evolved to eat raw scraps scavenged from carcasses, we as their modern human companions can do an awful lot better than simply feeding them the same subsistence diet they would get in the wild. To put it in other terms, would you prefer a modern cooked diet prepared using all the nutritional knowledge we've gained as an advanced society, or the same diet your stone-age ancestors used to eat (raw meat and vegetables)? Assuming the answer is a modern diet, then I hope you see the parallel for our dogs and the reason why we should not be persuaded by emotive arguments from the often passionate raw feeding lobby that only an ancestral diet will do.

So, if a raw diet is not the answer, then what is the best way to feed your dog? I believe that commercial pet foods offer the best solution to ensuring that your dog gets the correct combination of nutrients to maximise his long-term health. But, and it's a big but, there are commercial pet foods and commercial pet foods and it is vital that you choose an appropriate product for your dog. Too many are canine junk food, stuffed full of chemical additives and cheap ingredients that technically supply the nutrients your dog requires but only in the most basic and low-level way. If you want your dog to live to their full potential, then feeding a diet that does more than simply tick the boxes in terms of protein, carbohydrate and fat is vital.

As discussed in the section on puppy foods, there is a wide variety of ingredients that make up commercial dog foods, and it's important to understand how your dog can use the ingredients and how they will impact on his health. A figure of 26 per cent protein is all very well, but if that protein comes from poor-quality sources such as soya or vegetable extracts, or beef – which is more difficult for a dog to metabolise – the end result will not be as positive as if 26 per cent protein came from high-quality meats such as chicken or lamb. It's really important to not just choose a product based on the headline facts and figures on the front of the packet, but to turn the pack over and read the ingredients in detail. Only by doing this can you hope to really understand what's in the food, and therefore how appropriate it is for your dog.

Joe's Surgery Casebook

A SUMMONS TO THE ROYAL COLLEGE...

One of the things vets dread is the appearance of an official-looking letter on the doormat with the insignia of the Royal College of Veterinary Surgeons on the front. These letters are often routine, but there's always the fear at the back of your mind that one contains not a circular about elections for the new president or suchlike, but a summons to respond to a complaint from a client.

So it was with some trepidation that I opened a thick and unexpected letter bearing the RCVS logo one morning just before I left the house for surgery. As soon as I opened the letter my heart sank. I saw the dreaded words 'complaint of professional misconduct' at the top of the first page. Wracking my brains to think of anything I'd done that could have warranted such action, I scanned the letter and my fear quickly turned to confusion as I read the details of the complaint.

The complainant was not a client of my surgery, and was not somebody I'd ever met or had any professional dealings with, so the cause of her complaint was not based on any action I'd taken with respect to one of her pets, but something else entirely. This woman was complaining to the Royal College because of my pet-food company Pets' Kitchen which I'd set up to develop my own ranges of natural dog and cat foods. In her statement she claimed that by selling and promoting dry dog and cat foods I was causing harm and even death to thousands of pets. She believed passionately that feeding any commercial pet food, even those like my Pets' Kitchen foods which are natural and made from good-quality ingredients, was tantamount to physically assaulting a pet because the only healthy way to feed any animal was with a raw diet based on their ancestral diet.

As soon as I'd read the document I realised that there would be little to worry about as her views were clearly so much at odds with the veterinary and scientific communities. Indeed, the complaint was given short shrift by the Royal College. However, her passionate belief that prompted her to take the drastic step of reporting me to the Royal College for professional misconduct did make me realise quite how emotive this subject is to pet owners – and how important it is to get a logical and scientific argument across to counter such views.

THE CAMPAIGN FOR REAL PET FOOD

When I set up my own natural pet food company, Pets' Kitchen, I was convinced that the nation's pet owners would jump at the chance to buy high-quality natural foods for their cats and dogs. And while the foods certainly did prove to be popular with pets and their owners, I quickly realised that getting the message across about the benefits of natural food and raising awareness of the effects of artificial additives was not going to be as easy as I'd hoped.

After battling for a while and seeing several other small food companies producing pet foods free from artificial additives also struggling to get their message heard, I decided to set up a campaigning group to try to pool our resources and take a serious fight to the big boys of the pet-food industry. Our aim was simple – encourage pet owners to think about what they are feeding to their pets and consider the effects that artificial additives and low-quality ingredients might be having on their health.

With five companies supporting the campaign initially, we had an immediate impact, with lots of high-profile media coverage and thousands of visitors to our website. Before long, we saw that we were having an effect not just in terms of educating the consumer as we'd planned, but also within the industry itself. I was summoned to the headquarters of the Pet Food Manufacturers Association (PFMA) in London and quizzed on the campaign by representatives of the major multinational companies – all of which seemed to have a vested interest in retaining the industry status quo. It was an interesting discussion, but by the end there was little common ground between us. I had not changed my view that honest, natural food was the best approach for all pets, and the PFMA showed no sign that they would ever endorse my apparently revolutionary approach.

The campaign has become a great success and really helped to change attitudes in the pet world, with more and more people now being committed to feeding a healthy natural diet to their pets, which is wonderful. If you'd like to find out more, visit the campaign website at www.crpf.org.uk.

Commercial pet food does seem to stir up anxiety among pet owners. There are many misconceptions about this kind of feeding, which I think are well worth addressing. So here's my quick mythbuster's guide to commercial pet foods:

Cooking food destroys many of the nutrients – There is some truth to this, cooking does denature some proteins and break down some of the more fragile vitamins. However, cooking also has several very beneficial effects including making many more nutrients available to the digestive tract than if the food was raw, and releasing more energy from the food, making it more efficient as a food.

Extruded foods are the worst of all because the process involves such high temperatures and pressures – Extrusion is the process by which most commercial dry pet foods are made. A mix of ingredients is usually steam cooked under pressure and squeezed through holes in a metal plate (the extrusion process) before being chopped off by a rotating blade to form the individual kibbles. It is a fairly industrial process, with large hoppers, conveyor belts and great big extrusion vessels churning out tonnes of food every hour – but that doesn't mean that the food that comes out is unhealthy. In fact, extruded foods can be among the best pet foods available as the process is so carefully managed and the exact mix of nutrients in the final product is so precisely controlled. Obviously you can only get good-quality foods if you put in good-quality ingredients, and far too many extruded foods are not as good as they could be simply because of what goes into them – but it's not the process itself that's to blame. It is definitely possible to produce a top-quality natural extruded food that is free from artificial additives which delivers all the nutrients your pet needs, so long as the right ingredients are put into the machine. It's really very similar to processed human foods – there are lots which are very poor quality due to the nature of the ingredients that go in, but it is possible to get high-quality processed foods for people – you just have to pay for high-quality ingredients.

Processed foods are coated with poultry fat to make them edible – Often true, many dried pet foods are sprayed with fat after extrusion to improve the palatability and increase the fat content. This might not sound great, but, if you consider the end result rather than the process, a biscuit coated in a thin layer of oil is likely to be far more appealing to a pet than a dry biscuit. As we've previously discussed, fat is also an essential nutrient, and by adding it at the end of the process, after cooking, the pet gets the full benefit of the taste and fat-soluble vitamins it contains.

Baked pet foods are better than extruded – Baking is an alternative process to extruding and is popular with some pet owners who assume that it involves a gentler cooking process that will therefore produce a healthier end product. Instead of being cooked under pressure and forced through holes in an extruder, baked foods are formed as dollops of kibble dough which are then baked in a large gas-fired oven. As far as I'm aware, there is no evidence that this process produces foods that are healthier, but I can appreciate the view that it sounds better, with less physical processing, and I wouldn't rule out there being some small benefits to cooking food in this way.

However, there is a downside to baking and that's the energy costs. In these times of global warming and carbon footprints, we are all concerned about the energy costs associated with our food – and that of our pets as well. Baking uses significantly more energy than extrusion, making it a much less eco-friendly process. Although it may initially sound slightly better and some people would claim that baked foods are more palatable than extruded, the fact that baked foods will have a larger carbon footprint makes this process less appealing.

Commercial pet foods contain all sorts of unpleasant ingredients – chickens' feet and beaks, scrapings of the abattoir floor etc – I guess the answer to this one depends on your definition of 'unpleasant' – and of course on the quality of the food involved. It is true that most commercial pet foods use the leftovers from the human food chain, which includes mechanically recovered meat (meat pressure washed from the bones), viscera (heart, liver, intestines), chicken necks and wings, and some of the less popular cuts of meat. It is simply not economical to use prime chicken breast or leg of lamb in pet food, but this is not necessarily a bad thing for three good reasons. Firstly and most obviously is price. By using leftovers in this way pet food producers can make affordable products. If manufacturers were to use nothing but prime meat, the cost of pet-food would increase hugely.

The second advantage is a rather unexpected animal-welfare point. By using leftovers, pet-food companies are not directly increasing the number of animals slaughtered each year for food production. Instead, they are simply helping to make more efficient use of the animals we already rear and slaughter for our own consumption.

The final point is that, as we've already discussed, dogs and cats are natural scavengers and would normally eat the scraps of meat from a carcass and the intestines and other viscera, so the parts of animals that go into pet foods are those that our pets would naturally eat anyway. I realise that this might appear to counter my previous advice on raw food and my argument against feeding an 'evolutionary diet', but in this case I think there is a reasonable argument that feeding this kind of material is acceptable (though not necessarily optimum). Considering the other two points in addition make for a solid overall case.

Dogs and cats have no requirement for carbohydrate and, by feeding commercial foods which contain large amounts of carbohydrate, pet owners are causing serious health issues for their pets – This is simply untrue. There have been many scare stories about this subject and the internet is awash with unfounded allegations claiming that the feeding of carbohydrate to cats and dogs is responsible for all manner of diseases, including urinary diseases, diabetes, cancer and many others. However, none of these issues is backed up with any credible evidence, and a recent meta-analysis of all the data surrounding the issue of feeding carbohydrate to pets by Dr Tony Buffington of Ohio State University Hospital concluded, 'Current published evidence thus does not support a direct role for diet in general, and carbohydrates in particular, on disease risk in domestic cats.' Dr Buffington goes on to explain how genetic, environmental and lifestyle factors (such as indoor-only housing of cats) play a far more significant role in many of the diseases which are often implicated in carbohydrate-rich diets.

So I am happy that the scientific evidence strongly refutes any link between the feeding of carbohydrate to pets and health problems, and would recommend that this is not an area you should be worried about. It's far better to make sure the food you feed your dog is made with good-quality ingredients, including good-quality carbohydrates such as rice and oats, and is free from the artificial additives which we know can cause harm.

A final word on the emotive subject of commercial pet foods: if I could get one simple message across to every dog owner, it would be that of the importance of looking at the label so you can make an informed choice about what you feed your dog. To help with this, I've compiled an A–Z glossary of ingredients and terms commonly used on pet-food packaging, to help you see through the marketing blurb and really understand what's in each packet of food.

JOE'S A–Z PET FOOD GLOSSARY

Beef – Beef is a meat protein that is not ideal for pet dogs as it is harder to digest and utilise than other meats such as chicken and lamb. It can also cause dietary intolerances and allergies.

Brewer's Yeast – Dried brewer's yeast is a natural by-product of the brewing industry and is an excellent source of B-complex vitamins and amino acids.

Cellulose – Cellulose is a form of fibre derived from plants which can help stimulate the production of saliva, and theoretically assist the passage of hairballs.

Chicken (Fresh) – Fresh chicken is highly palatable, highly digestible and an excellent protein source for cats and dogs. It has an extremely high biological value meaning that it is easily broken down into its constituent amino acids (the building blocks of protein) necessary for a variety of structural and metabolic functions within the body. As previously mentioned, most fresh chicken used in pet foods is chicken viscera – so organ meat and intestines – rather than the juicy chicken breasts that manufacturers might prefer you to envisage. Fresh chicken contains much more moisture than dried chicken meal, so there will be less actual meat protein from fresh chicken compared to dried. Having said that, the benefits in terms of taste and nutritional value do make up for this, providing there is sufficient fresh chicken in the recipe (at least 26 per cent).

Chicken Meal – Like fresh chicken, chicken meal is an excellent protein source. It comprises the clean parts of the carcass ground up into a calcium-rich flour. Good-quality chicken meal (used in most pet foods) does not include heads, feet or feathers and is only made from chickens from the human food chain.

Chicken Fat/Oil – Chicken oil has a high and consistent level of the essential fatty acids that are necessary for a healthy skin and coat, and is considered to be one of the best-quality fat sources available. It is often sprayed on to dried kibbles to improve the palatability of a food.

Chondroitin Sulphate – Chondroitin is a natural supplement that blocks destructive enzymes that break down cartilage in the joint. There is always a low level of these destructive enzymes in the joint, but when injury or abnormal wear occurs the enzymes multiply. Chondroitin is considered to be completely safe, and any excess that is not required by the body is simply excreted in the urine. It is found in many preparations and supplements for dogs with arthritis, and increasingly also in foods. Just be aware that to be effective you need to be giving around 15–20mg per kilogram per day to your dog – so a 30kg Labrador will need between 450mg and 600mg per day. Moreover, the levels in many foods are very low indeed, so much so that they probably have little or no actual beneficial effect.

Corn – Corn (or maize as it is also known) is a starch carbohydrate. Ground corn is used as an energy source and is reasonably healthy, although generally not considered to be as suitable for dogs as rice and oats. Some people claim it can have a role in contributing to bowel disorders due to poorly digestible lectins, but there is little evidence to support this view.

Cranberry Extract – According to some scientific work and plenty of anecdotal evidence, cranberry extract may help in maintaining urinary tract health in dogs. It contains a sugar substance (D-mannose), which is able to prevent harmful bacteria from sticking to the mucosal walls, and also contains arbutin, which is effective against certain bacteria and fungi, including Candida. By limiting these harmful bacteria, cranberry extract is reported to be able to help reduce the incidence of conditions such as cystitis and bladder stones. Cranberry's antioxidant properties may also help to safeguard against the potentially harmful effects of free radicals.

Derivatives of Vegetable Origin – This is a general term used to describe by-products of vegetable origin, which can include anything that has been derived from a vegetable, from charcoal to compost! Seeing this ingredient in a pet food should set alarm bells ringing as it can be used to hide all manner of unspecified ingredients, such as residues, scraps and left-over peelings from vegetable-processing plants, which have very poor nutritional qualities.

EEC Permitted Additives – This term covers over 4,000 chemical additives that can be added to pet food without individually naming them. The list includes colours such as tartrazine and sunset yellow which have been proven to cause hyperactivity in children, and preservatives such as BHA which have been shown to have the potential to cause cancer in animals. Avoid like the plague!

Egg – Dried whole egg powder is a versatile ingredient. The yolk is a good fat source, while egg whites contain one of the purest forms of protein found in whole foods. Eggs are also a valuable source of vitamins and minerals.

Fish (Fresh) – Fresh fish such as salmon is a highly nutritious and palatable protein source for cats and dogs. It usually consists of the leftovers from human-grade fish, such as viscera, which is minced into a fine paste before being added to pet food. It contains fish oils, which are high in the health-promoting omega-3 very long-chain polyunsaturated fatty acids EPA and DHA, often simply referred to as 'omega-3s' – see 'Fish Oil' for more on this.

Fish (Meal) – Fish meal is the dried fish ingredient used in many pet foods, and is a natural balanced feed ingredient that is high in protein, energy and minerals, vitamins and micronutrients. It usually contains 6–10 per cent fish oil, so is a source of omega-3 fatty acids.

Fish Oil – Fish oil is included in dog-food recipes for energy, as a source of essential fatty acids and for the transport of the fat-soluble vitamins. Fish oil is an excellent source of omega-3 fatty acids, which in the human health context prevents or reduces the chances of developing coronary heart disease as well as reducing high blood pressure, and helping with kidney disorders, inflammatory bowel disorders and autoimmune disease. The fatty acids found in fish oils are essential to the growth and development of unborn and newly born babies and toddlers, and it is recommended that pregnant women, nursing mothers and babies should include oily fish or fish oil in their diets. With all this evidence of the benefits of these oils for people, it's no surprise that pet-food manufacturers are increasingly using fish oils in their recipes, which is great news. The only minor downside is the instance of fish taint that can arise if certain amounts of these oils are used, giving the food (and potentially the dog) a faint air of fishiness about them which is not usually desirable!

Glucosamine Sulphate – This is usually found together with chondroitin sulphate in joint supplements and some food recipes, and provides the building blocks to synthesise new joint cartilage. It is known to promote joint mobility and longevity, and has been shown to aid conditions such as hip dysplasia and arthritis. Like chondroitin, glucosamine is a safe and natural ingredient, and any excess that is not required by the body is simply excreted in the urine.

Grape Seed Extract – Grape seed extract is derived from the seeds of grapes used to make red wine. It is a source of oligomeric proanthocyanidins (OPCs), which are a category of bioflavenoids, water-soluble plant pigments that may support health by strengthening the blood capillaries and other connective tissue. Grape seed extract is also an extremely powerful antioxidant, and is possibly the only antioxidant with the capacity to cross into the brain from the bloodstream, thus improving mental alertness. As you may be aware (and certainly will be when you read the next section!), grapes themselves can be highly toxic to dogs, but grape seed extract is only ever included in pet foods at a safe level so don't panic if you see this on the ingredients panel as it won't have any harmful side effects.

Green Tea Extract – Derived from the plant Camellia sinesis, and unlike black tea, unfermented, green tea extract permits the active constituents to remain unaltered in the herb. It is a powerful antioxidant that supports the cardiovascular system. Traditional Chinese medicine has recommended green tea to aid digestion, enhance immunity and improve energy levels – so there's little doubt it will be beneficial to dogs as well as people, as the basic chemistry involved is identical in both species.

Lamb Meal – Lamb meal is rich in calcium. It is produced from meat trimmings and the clean parts of the carcass cooked, dried and ground into a fine flour. It does not include the wool, blood, head, hooves and specified risk material such as the spinal cord, and is a very healthy source of high-quality protein.

L-carnitine – L-carnitine is produced in small quantities in the body by the liver and testes. It is naturally present in meat, yeasts, egg and milk and increases fat metabolism in the skeletal and cardiac muscle, and is thought to possibly improve endurance and stamina. It also may be of benefit to the overweight or less active dog since it helps to increase the conversion of fat to energy and helps maintain lean body mass, so it is often found at higher levels in diet foods for dogs and those specifically targeted at obese animals.

Linseed – Linseed is also known as flax. This plant is a good source of dietary fibre, omega-3 fatty acids and lignans (which have antioxidant properties). Linseed oil contains linoleic acid and alpha linoleic acid. Linoleic acid is a polyunsaturated fatty acid used in the biosynthesis of prostaglandins and cell membranes.

Liver – The liver is a very nutritious source of good-quality protein as well as many vitamins including vitamins A, B, E, D and K and minerals including zinc, manganese, selenium and iron. It is not listed as an ingredient in most dried foods, although it may well be present, hidden under the 'meat and animal derivatives' term, but some natural wet foods use liver as a major ingredient.

Meat and Animal Derivatives – A loose term that covers any meat or animal by-product, without specifying what it is, or even what species it comes from! This term can be used to hide unhealthy or undesirable ingredients, such as low-quality by-products and less healthy meats such as beef. It also enables manufacturers to change the protein source with every batch without changing the label, a practice which is widespread because it allows manufacturers to use whatever meat is available at the lowest price at the time of production. It doesn't necessarily mean the food is unhealthy, but you simply don't know what you are feeding, so my advice would be to steer well clear of any foods that use this term on their ingredients declarations.

Methyl-sulfonyl-methane (MSM) – A naturally occurring form of organic sulphur derived from pine bark. It's reported beneficial properties include the relief of pain and inflammation. It is also thought that MSM may improve mental alertness and relieve stress, so it is popular in dog foods targeted at older animals.

Nucleotides – These natural short-chain proteins (derived from yeast) are able to enhance metabolic function and have particular benefits to the digestive and immune systems. Nucleotides allow optimum levels of nutrients to be absorbed by the body, as well as facilitating a more rapid cell replication in response to an outside challenge, aiding tissue recovery and healing.

Oats – Oats are a good source of energy and protein, as well as being rich in fat, minerals and vitamins E and B.

Pork – Pork is not widely used in dog foods for several historical reasons to do mainly with the supply chain and worries over certain parasitic diseases that can be passed on through pork meat such as hydatid cysts. However, pork is an excellent meat for dogs, and contains more of the essential amino acids than other meats. Lean pork is one of the most digestible protein sources. It is also hypoallergenic and low in nitrates, and antibiotic and hormone free.

Pork-based dog food is becoming very popular for sled, hunting and performance dogs because of the type of protein base needed for the high demands of these animals. I wouldn't be surprised if we start to see more pork-based foods becoming available in the future.

Potato – A generally healthy carbohydrate source that is often combined with salmon to provide an alternative to the usual chicken and rice or lamb and rice varieties for dogs that have allergies or intolerances to these foods. There are some concerns about a potential carcinogen called acrylamide which is present in potato but it is not considered to be a significant problem in processed dog foods.

Prebiotics – These are complex sugars that serve as a nutritional basis for probiotics. These complex sugars are not broken down by the normal digestive process and are also defined as 'non-digestible fibre'. The theory goes that when added to the diet they increase the chances of beneficial bacteria growing and thriving in the intestine.

In dog food, the most common prebiotics are beet pulp (in moderate amounts, otherwise it's just a filler) and chicory root extract. Chicory contains inulin, a form of dietary fibre, which contains oligosaccharides that are thought to promote the growth of beneficial intestinal bacteria. Using the same arguments that are used by proponents of probiotics, fans of prebiotics claim that high levels of 'friendly' intestinal bacteria can help to improve digestion, decrease disease and strengthen the immune system.

Probiotics – Probiotics are the so-called 'good' bacteria added after the cooking process which are used to seed the intestinal populations of bacteria and promote good digestive health. There are many claimed benefits to probiotics including boosting the immune system; improving digestion; controlling yeast overgrowth; removing toxins from the body; helping manufacture B vitamins and promoting proper elimination. While they almost certainly can help in some of these areas, I would take any claim with a slight pinch of salt as there is often less rigorous scientific proof behind the claims than the manufacturers would have you believe.

Rabbit – A good source of high-quality protein, which is also suitable for allergic dogs who react to the more commonly used protein sources. Rabbit is not particularly popular due mainly to the slight squeamishness of dog owners who don't like to think of their dogs eating poor defenceless bunnies (but are quite happy for them to eat poor defenceless chickens!) but it is a perfectly suitable protein to consider.

Rice – Rice is a very digestible energy source and is often used as the main source of carbohydrate in pet foods. Brown rice, which retains the husk, is higher in fibre so is generally considered to be healthier than the more processed white rice.

Rosemary Extract – Natural pet foods are often stabilised naturally using mixed tocopherols (which include vitamin E) and rosemary as alternatives to artificial chemicals such as BHA and BHT which have been linked to serious health problems in pets. Rosemary is a natural antioxidant and is primarily used to prevent the oxidisation of the fat components of diets.

Seaweed – Seaweed, or kelp, might sound like a strange ingredient for your dog to eat, but it is a useful source of minerals including sodium, potassium, calcium and iodine and is entirely natural.

Soya – Although often touted as a healthy foodstuff for humans, soya protein is hard to digest and utilise and not a good-quality ingredient for dogs. It has also been associated with dietary intolerances and allergies, so I would recommend avoiding foods containing soya.

Spirulina – Spirulina is a one-celled form of blue-green algae that thrives in warm, alkaline fresh-water bodies. Spirulina is often thought of as the 'food of the future' because of its ability to synthesise high-quality concentrated food more efficiently than any other algae. Spirulina is 65 to 71 per cent complete protein, with all essential amino acids in perfect balance, whereas, in comparison, beef is only 22 per cent protein. Spirulina also provides high concentrations of many other nutrients – vitamin B12, amino acids, chelated minerals, pigmentations, rhamnose sugars (complex natural plant sugars), trace elements, enzymes and the rare essential fatty acid gamma-linolenic acid (GLA). The main downside is the price – it costs around £4,000 per tonne and so any beneficial amounts in dog food are likely to significantly increase the cost.

Sugar Beet Pulp – Beet pulp is a by-product of sugar production and a good source of both soluble and insoluble fibre. The soluble fibre is a good food source for the friendly bacteria in the large intestine, and also slows the rate of food passage through the gut which provides more time for the digestive process to take place, maximising the absorption of nutrients from food. The insoluble fibre increases peristalsis (the movement of the bowels), helps an animal to feel satisfactorily full and provides a crunchy texture to the kibbles which can help keep the teeth clean.

In general, fibre is important for maintaining normal intestinal function, and, as you've probably noticed, dogs with stomach upsets can often be found eating grass or other vegetation, which some people put down to an attempt to soothe their gut with increased fibre. A balanced diet containing the right amount of fibre may also reduce the incidence of conditions such as diabetes mellitus and obesity, as well as helping to prevent constipation and diarrhoea, so it's a vital ingredient to consider.

Tocopherols (TCP) – Natural pet foods are often preserved naturally using tocopherols (vitamin E), as all dry pet foods require an antioxidant in order to prevent the fat components in the diet from becoming rancid on exposure to air, and, as mentioned under Rosemary Extract, tocopherols and rosemary provide a good natural alternative to chemicals such as BHA and BHT.

Venison – Meat from deer is a very good source of protein, and also tends to be fairly low in fat, particularly saturated fats, unlike other meats. Venison is also rich in iron and B vitamins, and is generally a very healthy meat for dogs to eat.

Yucca Extract – Yucca schidigera extracts are from a plant in the Lily family that is native to the southwestern United States and Mexico. Native Americans have used Yucca for hundreds of years to treat a variety of disorders, as it is rich in iron, magnesium, manganese, phosphorus, selenium and silicon, as well as vitamins A, B and C. Yucca has antioxidant properties and is thought that it might help reduce faecal and body odour in dogs – which is a good thing!

Wheat – This is a good source of carbohydrate and protein, but it is one of the main ingredients known to cause dietary intolerances and allergies, so should be avoided when feeding pets with these problems.

HOME-COOKING FOR YOUR DOG

As previously mentioned in the chapter on puppyhood, I am a great believer in home-cooking as part of a healthy diet for dogs. I don't see it as a viable alternative to commercial foods for day-to-day feeding, but instead as something special that gives you and your dog pleasure, as well as contributing to their long-term health. By cooking a meal for your dog, you are devoting time and attention to him, as well as giving him a nutritious treat, and this combination of positive messages will only serve to reinforce his devotion and 'love' for you. In short, cooking for your dog is a great way to strengthen your relationship with him.

In this section I'm going to look at the details of home-cooking – the ingredients you can and can't use, and then present a selection of my favourite recipes for you to try at home.

The first thing to say is that the vast majority of the ingredients you use when cooking for yourself and your family are perfectly suitable for cooking meals for your dog. Dogs are the ultimate digestive dustbins and can really cope with pretty much everything we can offer them (with a few specific exceptions which I'll discuss shortly). As long as you're not trying to feed your dog on a home-cooked diet every day, you can be pretty flexible and imaginative with the ingredients you use. The only problem you're likely to confront in most cases is digestive upsets caused by a change in diet, which can lead to quite severe diarrhoea in dogs with sensitive digestive tracts. If your dog does have a delicate constitution, home-cooking is probably not for him and you'd be better sticking to a dull but safe routine of a commercial diet that you know he copes with rather than trying to liven things up with home-cooking. Many dogs that have been used to an exclusively commercial diet for many years will struggle to cope with home-cooked meals initially, but if you gradually persist you often find that their digestive tracts can adapt to the change in diet and enable them to cope with a wider range of food after a while. The tricky thing is deciding whether your dog is one of those who just needs a little time to get used to a varied diet or whether he is an animal with dietary intolerances or allergies and therefore unable to cope with a mixed diet.

It's worth a quick digression at this point to discuss dietary intolerances and allergies because it seems that more and more dogs are being diagnosed with an intolerance or allergy these days (whether or not that's due to a real rise in cases or better diagnosis is hard to ascertain). The first thing to clear up is the difference between the two conditions. Although they are often mentioned in the same breath, they are completely different conditions with very different causes and effects.

A dietary intolerance is simply the inability of a dog to digest a particular foodstuff, whether it is a particular type of protein or other ingredient. The usual end result of an intolerance is diarrhoea whenever the dog eats a food containing the ingredient in question, which can end up being severe and debilitating. It is usually resolved very quickly once the diet is changed.

A food allergy on the other hand is a more complex disorder that involves the immune system reacting to a particular food, usually a specific type of protein. The end result of a food allergy is not usually diarrhoea or vomiting, although these can happen, but symptoms affecting other parts of the body, most notably the skin. It might sound strange for a food allergy to manifest itself in the skin, but the immune system runs throughout the body, and a reaction started by a protein over-stimulating the immune system in the gut can easily have effects throughout the body. The most common symptoms of a food allergy tend to be itchiness and inflammation of the skin. It can become a very severe problem that causes long-term health issues for the dog.

The main problem when dealing with a food allergy is making a diagnosis because the symptoms of allergic skin disease caused by a food are identical to those we see in dogs with different types of allergy, most commonly allergies to inhaled allergens such as pollens (a condition called atopy). Differentiating between a food allergy and atopy by looking at the dog alone is almost impossible, so vets have to use a variety of tests and techniques to distinguish between the two conditions. The first approach is to test specifically for atopic allergies using blood tests to look at the levels of certain antibodies in the blood, or skin tests which show how much the body reacts when certain allergens are injected into the skin. This enables us to indentify allergies to certain allergens such as pollens, housedust mites, parasites such as fleas and so on, but the results are not always 100 per cent accurate or clear – and don't necessarily rule out a food allergy as a concurrent issue.

The only way to diagnose – or rule out – a food allergy is to undertake what's known as an exclusion trial. This is where the dog is fed exclusively on a 'hypoallergenic' diet which is free from all the ingredients known to commonly cause allergies (such as beef, wheat, soya and dairy ingredients) for a period of around six weeks. During this time the owner assesses the dog's skin condition to see if the change of diet has made any difference. If there has been an improvement, the diagnosis is confirmed by changing the dog back on to their previous diet, and observing the recurrence of the symptoms. This complete trial will have then proved beyond reasonable doubt that something in the dog's original diet was responsible for the skin problem, and that by changing to a hypoallergenic diet the problem is resolved.

It's worth at this stage mentioning a few things about hypoallergenic diets. The term 'hypoallergenic' really means very little as all it really says is that the food is 'less allergenic' than other foods – it doesn't mean that the food is guaranteed to be free from anything that could cause an allergy, as that's an impossible claim to make. After all, pretty much any ingredient could theoretically cause an allergy. However, most diets marketed as hypoallergenic are free from the main allergens involved in canine skin disease, and work well in the majority of food-allergy cases. There are some dogs, however, who have such severe food allergies that they still react to these standard low-allergy foods, and for these dogs there are some very clever new foods on the market specifically engineered to minimise the chances of a reaction. I use the word 'engineered' in this context as these foods really are works of scientific engineering rather than culinary creations – instead of containing normal proteins which are the conventional cause of allergic reaction, these foods contain hydrolysed proteins which are essentially normal protein molecules broken down into tiny fragments. These small pieces of protein are too small for the immune system to react to, so it can't trigger a food-allergy reaction. Often sold only by vets, these foods can be highly effective and are often the only solution in severe cases, but this kind of technology doesn't come cheap, so be aware that, if you have to go down this route, your dog-food bills are probably going to be higher than your own!

Joe's Pets

JACK'S DILEMMA

My dog Jack loves his food. His favourite dinner of all is my own recipe Joe & Jack's Lamb and Rice dried food which was named in his honour after he helped me develop it. However, over the months that I was working on perfecting the recipe, and Jack was tasting and testing various different versions of the kibbles, I began to realise that he was suffering from intermittent diarrhoea. He's a very clean and discreet dog who always runs off to go to the toilet out of sight whenever possible, so it was hard initially to really see the problem. Over the months it became clear that Jack was suffering from quite bad bouts of diarrhoea.

I tried various treatments but it was only when I moved on to trialling a new chicken and rice recipe that his problem cleared up – and it was then that I realised that Jack was most likely to be suffering from an intolerance to something in the lamb and rice recipe. Sure enough, whenever I tried him again on the lamb and rice food, the same problem recurred, which confirmed the diagnosis.

So poor old Jack is now faced with the miserable situation of not being allowed to eat his favourite recipe, and the one that he was instrumental in creating, which is a real shame for him – but better this than suffering from chronic diarrhoea. Still, he doesn't suffer too much as the chicken and rice recipe seems to go down very well, so don't feel too sorry for him!

The vast majority of the ingredients in your kitchen will be fine for your dog – meat, pasta, rice, most vegetables, bread, fish and so on, and there are also a few perhaps more unexpected ingredients that work really well for dogs, including:

- Fruit – Going back to the evolutionary diet argument (it's one I like to use when it suits my point of view!), it's likely that, in the wild, dogs would have scavenged windfall fruit as well as digesting the remains of fruit eaten by other animals when they pick over the carcass, so giving your dog fruit is not as strange as it might sound. Fresh fruit is packed full of antioxidants, vitamins and all sorts of other healthy nutrients, so it's great for keeping your dog in top condition.
- Yoghurt – Live yoghurt in particular is a great food for dogs due to the probiotic bacteria it contains, which also makes it perfect for dogs with digestive upsets. Yoghurt is also a great source of protein, calcium and vitamins, so it's an all-round winner for your dog!
- Cottage cheese – Another surprisingly healthy dairy food which is great for growing puppies and lactating bitches.

On the other side of the equation, there are a few potential dangers posed by certain ingredients that you should be aware of before you get started in the canine kitchen, and these are:

- Tomatoes – They might sound like an unlikely danger and certainly a small amount of ripe tomato is unlikely to cause any problems, but green tomatoes can cause

serious stomach upsets and even heart problems, so it's best to avoid them when cooking for your dog.

- Onions (and garlic) – These vegetables can cause blood problems including anaemia. Again, small amounts are very unlikely to cause any problems, but to be on the safe side I only use small amounts of garlic and very little onion in my recipes.
- Grapes and raisins – Both can cause very serious illness including kidney problems, and large amounts have been known to be fatal to dogs, so avoid wherever possible. As previously mentioned, grape seed extract is perfectly safe as an ingredient in commercial pet food.
- Chocolate – The dangers of chocolate to dogs are relatively well known, but it's worth reinforcing the point here as dogs do sadly die every year after eating chocolate. The problem is caused by a substance found in chocolate called theobromine (which is related to caffeine) that some dogs react very badly to, showing signs such as hyper-excitability, increased heart rate and muscle tremors. Dark chocolate contains the most theobromine and so is more dangerous to dogs than milk chocolate, but all forms of chocolate should be considered a danger to dogs. Having said all that, it is worth keeping the problem in perspective as a small nibble of chocolate is highly unlikely to cause any life-threatening problems – a Labrador-sized dog would need to ingest several hundred grams of dark chocolate to be at any real risk of dangerous complications.

• Mushrooms – Best avoided as some dogs do not tolerate mushrooms well and they can cause serious toxicity.

It's time to get down to some recipes. I've got a selection of meals for you to try, including some everyday meals, some for dogs with specific needs such as old age or health conditions, and one that you can even enjoy with your dog!

CHICKEN AND RICE

This recipe is one of the first I ever cooked for Jack and is still one of his favourites. It combines one of the healthiest proteins available – chicken – with rice which is an easily digestible carbohydrate, and a mixture of vegetables to provide lots of vitamins and minerals. It's great for all dogs, including those with sensitive digestions and older dogs, and is a recipe I often recommend for dogs with digestive upsets and diarrhoea. It's also ideal for freezing, so you can store it in single-serving-sized bags and then simply defrost a tasty and healthy meal the next time you want to give the dog something special.

Ingredients
   225g chicken mince
   200g rice (preferably brown)
   1 small carrot, finely grated (no need to peel the carrots, just make sure they are well scrubbed)
   150g fresh peas (or frozen peas will do if fresh are out of season)
   1 tsp yeast extract (such as Marmite)

Method

Boil the rice in a large pan of boiling water. When the rice is almost cooked (1–2 minutes before it's ready), add the grated carrot and peas to the water and simmer until the rice is done. This makes the vegetables much more digestible, without losing their goodness. Drain well.

Meanwhile, fry the mince for a few minutes until it is browned – you shouldn't need to add any oil as there is plenty of fat in the mince. Add the mince to the rice. Mix in the yeast extract. Serve when cooled.

LIVER DUMPLINGS IN A MARROWBONE GRAVY

This is another great recipe for dogs of all ages, as it is packed full of the goodness of liver, including vitamin A which is vital for eyesight, and minerals such as iron. Too much raw liver can cause health problems, but these cooked dumplings are ideal as a weekly treat, added to your dog's everyday dried food.

Ingredients
  100g breadcrumbs
  A little hot water
  200g beef or chicken liver, diced finely
  1 beaten egg
  1 large meaty marrowbone (or 2 stock cubes)
  25g flour
  25g butter

Method

Soften the breadcrumbs with just enough hot water to make them sticky, and then mix in the diced liver and beaten egg. Leave this to stand for half an hour so that it becomes firm.

Meanwhile, carefully place a large meaty marrowbone in a big pan of boiling water and let it simmer for about 45 minutes (alternatively, mix 2 stock cubes with 1.5 litres of boiling water).

Moisten your hands and shape the liver mixture into small round dumplings. Drop these into the simmering stock and cook uncovered for 15 minutes. Remove and leave to cool.

To make the gravy, melt the butter in a small pan. Add the flour and heat gently until it forms a rich brown paste. Add half a pint of the stock from the marrowbone/stock pot and stir over a medium heat for 5 minutes.

Once they have cooled, serve your dog a dumpling or two with his dried food and pour over a generous helping of gravy.

CHICKEN, SPINACH AND SARDINE MASH

(this will provide about two meals for a medium-sized dog)

This recipe is specifically designed for older dogs who particularly benefit from the easily digestible proteins from the chicken and the good-quality carbohydrate from the sweet potato. With added vitamins from the spinach and essential omega-3 oils from the sardines, this is a really healthy – and tasty – treat for an older dog.

Ingredients

    400g sweet potatoes

    250g chicken mince

    250g spinach, shredded

    1 tin sardines in oil

    $^1/_2$ teaspoon eggshell powder or 1 x 1000mg calcium supplement, crushed

    1 teaspoon brewer's yeast (from most health-food shops, often in tablet form that you can grind up into a powder)

Method

Cut the sweet potatoes into equal-sized pieces and then boil them in their skins until tender (about 10 minutes), and then drain and mash in a large mixing bowl.

While the sweet potatoes are cooking, gently fry the chicken mince without adding any fat, until it is cooked through (this will take about 5–7 minutes). Then add in the spinach and cook until wilted.

Add the sardines, along with all the oil, to the mince and spinach, and then transfer this mixture to the mixing bowl and combine with the mashed potato.

If you're using the eggshell powder, all you need to do is boil an egg, remove the shell and grind it up in a pestle and mortar – this provides an excellent natural source of calcium and the grittiness of the powder also helps keep your dog's teeth clean. Add the powder, or ground-up calcium supplement (if you're cheating!), followed by the brewer's yeast. Leave to cool and then form the mixture into egg-sized balls.

Serve on their own or with a sprinkling of your dog's normal dried biscuits.

CHICKEN SOUP FOR THE SICKLY DOG

This recipe is designed to help your dog back to good health if they're a bit below par, or recovering from something more serious such as an operation. It's full of goodness from the chicken and vegetables, and is easily digestible, nourishing and tasty – just what your dog needs if he's not at his best.

Ingredients
  2 chicken drumsticks
  1 carrot, chopped (no need to peel, just make sure it's scrubbed thoroughly)
  1 potato, chopped into medium-sized pieces
  1 teaspoon parsley, chopped
  1 stock cube

Method
Masterchef this recipe is not. All you need to do is cover the chicken and vegetables with boiling water and simmer on a

low heat for 30 minutes. Remove the chicken from the pan, discard the bones and return the meat to the pan. Sprinkle in the parsley and serve slightly warm, with a natural dried food sprinkled in as croutons.

SAUSAGE AND LENTIL CASSEROLE

This is one of my recipes that I created for dog owners to share with their dogs. This might sound a bit strange, and go against what I've said about feeding your dog separately from yourself to ensure there's a clear separation in your dog's mind between his food and human food – but, provided you feed your dog at a different time and in a different place to yourself and the rest of the family, there's no reason why you can't enjoy the same home-cooked recipe.

This is probably my favourite recipe of all and it's a great dish for you and the dog to share on a cold winter's evening after a long walk. Lentils are not a bad food for dogs, but they are not totally nutritionally balanced (and can cause wind!) so this is a dish best fed occasionally rather than every day. Reserve it for a particularly wet and cold evening when you both need cheering up with something warm and tasty.

This recipe should make about six servings for a medium-sized dog.

Ingredients
  6 sausages
  1 teaspoon olive oil
  1 small leek, finely chopped
  2 garlic cloves, crushed
  150g Puy lentils

600ml chicken stock
1 teaspoon balsamic vinegar
3 tablespoons chopped parsley
Salt and pepper

Method
Heat the olive oil in a large deep pan.

Fry the sausages in the olive oil for 7–8 minutes until browned all the way around. Add the chopped leek and garlic and cook for a further 5 minutes. Next, add the lentils and hot stock. Bring to the boil and simmer gently for 45 minutes, until the lentils are tender and most of the stock has been absorbed. Finally, add the vinegar and parsley, and season with salt and pepper to taste.

Eat yours while it's still piping hot, but make the dog wait until it has cooled down before spooning out a couple of sausages and sauce into his bowl.

Joe's TV Casebook

LIVE CANINE CUISINE ON THE BBC!
When I look back over my TV career, one of my favourite memories will be of the occasion I turned into a TV chef and cooked up my sausage and lentil casserole recipe live on the BBC. The show was called *Animal Rescue Live* and was presented by my old *Blue Peter* colleague Matt Baker and

Selina Scott. It was filmed at Battersea Dogs Home in South London, and included all sorts of features from heart-rending stories of maltreated and abandoned pets to celebrities dancing with dogs – plus eccentric vets cooking up meals for dogs!

The recipe I chose was one of my favourites – sausage and lentil casserole. After demonstrating how to cook the meal and discussing the main dos and don'ts of cooking for your dog, I produced the finished dish at the end of the show where it was sampled, not only by a couple of the Battersea canine residents, but also by Matt and Selina. Thankfully it went down well with everyone. From the correspondence I received afterwards, it was also a hit with the viewers, many of whom got in touch to say how much they and their dogs enjoyed the recipe when they tried it at home.

To date that's been my one and only venture into TV cookery, but you never know, if the concept of cookery for pets catches on, you could see me with my own cookery show for pets one of these days...

SIX

Relationship Problems

So far in *Your Dog and You* we've mainly considered how to build and maintain a good relationship with your dog, but now it is time to consider what happens when this relationship breaks down and behaviour problems arise.

The first point to emphasise is that all behavioural problems, with the possible exception of those very rare problems caused by medical conditions, are a direct product of the relationship between owner and dog. Like it or not, we control our dog's behaviour as clearly as we do their physical health and wellbeing. When we build a healthy and happy relationship with our dog, based on our own and our dog's needs and circumstances as outlined earlier in this book, there will be no reason for behavioural problems to arise. If, however, a relationship is flawed from the start, or circumstances change and cause the relationship to deteriorate as a result, the end result is nearly always a behavioural problem such as aggression, anxiety or fear.

The main behavioural problems that occur in dogs, and that we will cover in this chapter are:

- Inappropriate behaviours
- Fears and phobias
- Compulsions and hyperactivity
- Aggression

INAPPROPRIATE BEHAVIOURS

The term 'inappropriate behaviours' describes, as the name suggests, those behaviours that we the owners consider to be inappropriate or unsuitable. They are not necessarily behaviours that are inherently wrong, but are often just the right behaviour in the wrong place or misguided responses to certain situations. The classic examples of this kind of behavioural problem include puppies (and adult dogs) going to the toilet in the wrong place, destructive behaviour and various 'eating disorders' such as scavenging and coprophagia (eating poo!).

The first problem to look at is probably the most common: inappropriate toilet activity, specifically weeing or pooing indoors. This is most common in puppies who are learning the house rules about where is and where is not an appropriate place to go to the toilet, but it can also be an issue in older dogs who either relapse for some reason or never quite get the hang of toilet training in the first place.

The reasons behind inappropriate toilet activity are, like many behavioural issues, usually down to the owner and our relationship with our dog. Most common house-training problems are caused by fear, distraction, poorly thought-out punishment regimes or simply poor house training in the first place. All of these issues are owner problems rather than dog problems. When confronted with a puppy or adult dog who is having difficulty in this way, make sure you remember that it is much more likely to be you at fault than your dog. Domestic dogs learn everything they know from their owners and extended human families so we have to take responsibility when things go wrong. It is important to remember this when trying to fix a problem such as inappropriate toilet activity as it is crucial if you are to understand the issues that have caused the problem and be able to resolve them.

So, if your dog is weeing and pooing in inappropriate places, how can you work out what's caused the problem and do something about it? There are several common causes for inappropriate urination and defecation, so you need to look at your dog's behaviour and see which of those causes is most likely. For example, if your puppy is obviously nervous and fearful when placed outside and runs back indoors to empty his bladder, it's highly likely that he is suffering from fear-induced inappropriate urination, probably caused by poor socialisation with the great outdoors when he was younger. Resolving this kind of problem involves gradual desensitisation and retraining so he gradually comes to associate being outdoors with pleasurable emotions and becomes comfortable going to the toilet outside. It can take a while to accomplish this, but the techniques you need are exactly those already described in the training section, so it is usually perfectly possible to succeed given a little patience and perseverance.

Distraction is a less common problem but can lead to particularly inquisitive puppies spending so much time investigating their environment that they forget all about going for a wee and only remember when they are less excited and distracted back at home. The solution for this kind of problem is to take your puppy to the same spot at the start of a walk, day in day out, so they don't get excited until after they've had this chance to go to the toilet – only take them somewhere new and exciting once they've been for a wee.

Inappropriate punishment regimes can be more serious and are a classic example of a relationship problem causing a behavioural problem. If you have used too much negative conditioning during toilet training – shouting at your puppy when they wee indoors and so on – then he might become so traumatised that he is terrified of urinating in your presence, irrespective of location. So even outdoors, where he knows he's supposed to go for a wee, he's simply too scared that you might shout at him to go so he holds it in until he gets home where he can slink off into a corner out of sight and relieve himself – at which point you catch him in the act and shout at him again and the vicious cycle continues.

Curing a problem like this requires you to really reconsider your approach to training and the basics of your relationship with your dog. Try to focus more on positive rewards as a way of modifying your dog's behaviour rather than negative punishments and you should be able to gradually remove the negative associations and fears that have built up and allow your dog to grow confident that weeing outside is the right thing to do and brings positive rewards for him.

Poor house training in the first place is obviously another potential cause of inappropriate toilet activity. It is a very common problem which overlaps with punishment regimes. Another typical example of poor house training which can lead to problems is the use of paper in the house when a puppy is being trained. Many people use newspaper on the floor as part of their toilet-training programme, allowing the puppy to go to the toilet on the paper in the house before teaching them to go outside. This is all very well in theory and I'm not denying the practical advantages in terms of controlling mess, but the main problem with this approach is that it can teach the puppy that it's OK to go to the toilet inside the house. Despite the fact that you think you are teaching them that it's only OK to go in the house if it's on that specific bit of newspaper by the back door, the message your puppy takes away might be slightly different. This subtle difference in interpretation is all that's needed to cause a big problem later on. So my advice would be to never use paper when toilet training your dog. If you have done so and you have a problem with inappropriate toilet activity later on, then you will need to go through a process of retraining using positive rewards to make it clear to your dog that he got the wrong end of the stick when you first trained him and it's not OK to go to the toilet in the house under any circumstances!

The final reason for inappropriate toilet activity is an

aversion to bad weather – some dogs really hate going for a wee outside when it's raining. To overcome this kind of problem, you need to start by finding an outdoor area that your dog is happy to use when it's wet, such as a covered area, and then gradually introduce locations as the dog becomes more used to going to the toilet in all kinds of weather. It may not be a common problem, but it can be very frustrating for all concerned – it's bad enough having a wet smelly dog in the house when it's pouring with rain outside, but, if that wet smelly dog then empties his bladder in the kitchen because he didn't fancy weeing outside in the rain, you are going to get pretty fed up!

Joe's Surgery Casebook

HARVEY AND THE CAT!

While thinking about the subject of dogs that refused to go to the toilet outside, one particular case from many years ago came to mind. It involved a young Spaniel called Harvey who suddenly started going to the toilet in the house after being perfectly well toilet trained as a puppy. After a few weeks of Harvey weeing in the house nearly every day, his owner brought him in to see me in a state of near desperation.

'I just don't know what to do,' explained Mrs Simpson, shaking her head at Harvey who stood, trembling on the consulting-room table. 'It started suddenly, and now he simply refuses to go out into the garden and do his business. If I put him out, he just waits by the back door, whining, until I let him in – and then he goes and wees in the hall or the lounge when I'm not looking. I've tried everything – leaving him outside for hours, telling him off for weeing inside – but it's just getting worse and I'm at my wit's end!'

Solving Harvey's problem took a bit of detective work but after a little while talking to Mrs Simpson the key to what was going on became clear. Harvey was petrified of a big new ginger cat that had moved in next door a month previously and was patrolling their garden. This fear of the cat had then been exacerbated by Mrs Simpson's attempts to resolve the problem by leaving him outside, which only served to fuel his fears, and telling him off when he went inside, which made him feel bad about going for a wee anywhere near his owner.

Once we'd understood the cause of the problem, resolving it wasn't too hard – I advised Mrs Simpson to arm herself with a large water pistol and do her best to chase the cat away to make Harvey less scared of being outside, and to get him used to weeing outside again by taking him for walks to do his business rather than letting him out into the garden.

It took a few weeks, but it did work and, by the time I saw Harvey again for his booster, all was well and there had been no more problems – which just goes to show that the theory really does work in practice!

Destructive behaviours are the next type of inappropriate behaviours to consider. These kinds of problems are particularly common in puppies, where the issue is not usually the chewing or digging itself (as this is a normal behaviour that all puppies engage in) but rather the fact that such activities are inappropriately directed. Common targets for inappropriate chewing include household items such as shoes and clothes, which have an obvious value to you the owner, and things they shouldn't be chewing because they are potentially dangerous to the puppy, such as electrical wires or objects that might be swallowed and cause choking or an intestinal obstruction.

The first thing to mention is how important chewing is to puppies. Chewing, digging and exploring are all essential behavioural activities that help shape the minds and bodies of dogs, and we need to ensure that we allow our puppies to indulge in these activities as they grow. As well as providing physical and mental stimulation, chewing itself also has direct physiological effects including stimulating the release of insulin, so we cannot simply prevent puppies from chewing – we just have to make sure we control what they chew and when.

Having said that chewing is a normal behaviour, it can also become an abnormal one rather than just inappropriate. Puppies that suffer fear or anxiety or have restricted exercise or social interaction can display exaggerated chewing and destructive behaviours, which are also often inappropriate in nature. These combined abnormal and inappropriate destructive behaviours are usually the most challenging to deal with.

Resolving inappropriate destructive behaviour is not easy, therefore, as with all behavioural issues, prevention is the key – the key to prevention is a good relationship between owner and dog. If you have built up a healthy relationship with your puppy so they do not feel stressed or anxious, and there are no uncertainties over ground rules and pack hierarchy, it should be easy to prevent inappropriate chewing and other destructive behaviours with simple steps including the provision of suitable items to chew, and discouraging any inappropriate behaviours as soon as they appear. If, however, your relationship with your dog is not a good one, then these kinds of behavioural problems will be much more likely – and harder to resolve.

Joe's Surgery Casebook

THINGS I'VE REMOVED FROM INSIDE DOGS

There are some cases in a vet's life that seem to happen once a year, every year – the cat trapped in the car engine compartment, the dog with a stick jammed in his mouth and so on. These cases are unusual, but seem to happen on a regular basis (if that makes any sense). As a newly qualified vet you are amazed the first time you see one of these cases, but then, after seeing one or two every year, it becomes less of a surprise and more of a case of 'Oh no, here we go again!'

Recently I saw my seemingly annual case involving a dog and a missing rubber toy. I think I've seen a case like this pretty much every year since I qualified back in 1996, and, despite this, I am always surprised by what I end up removing from inside dogs' intestines. One year it was an entire bouncing ball, another it was half a rubber bone – and this year the missing rubber object was a large round toy that the patient in question, a four-year-old Collie called Sam, had devoured over the course of a weekend.

'He's a real devil for chewing his toys,' explained Sam's owner apologetically. 'I'm always having to grab things from him. He nearly swallowed an entire tennis ball last year!'

This time though it seemed as though Sam had been a little too quick for her and half of the toy was unaccounted for, presumed swallowed.

'Every time he eats it's just coming straight back up,' said Sam's owner as I palpated his abdomen, 'and he's getting really miserable.'

'I can feel something inside,' I replied, 'and it is probably the missing toy I'm afraid, in which case he'll almost certainly need an operation to remove it.'

An x-ray quickly confirmed that the lump in Sam's abdomen was indeed the missing toy, a situation which left us little choice but to operate and remove it surgically. If left inside, there was a slim chance that it would work its way through and out the other end, but more probably it would remain stuck in place and cause potentially life-threatening complications.

The surgery required to remove a 'foreign body' such as this is generally fairly straightforward – and very rewarding. It is one of those instances when you know that the operation will completely cure the patient if it goes well. In Sam's case, the remains of the toy were lodged in his small intestine and the operation to remove it went very well, which was a great relief.

Aside from factors related to your relationship with your dog, the single most important thing you can do to prevent inappropriate chewing problems is to provide suitable toys for your puppy to chew on. There are literally thousands of chew toys on the market, so choosing the right one for your dog can be quite a daunting and confusing process. Here are my top tips for selecting the right toy for your dog:

1. A toy must be well made, well designed and safe –
   avoid cheap plastic toys that tend to fall apart and
   can pose a health risk if pieces are swallowed.
2. It must keep your puppy's attention – simple nylon

bones may be safe but they are also boring and unlikely to hold your puppy's attention, especially if there are more interesting alternatives, such as slippers! Rope toys or hollow rubber toys into which small morsels of food can be inserted are generally better at keeping a puppy interested.

3. Avoid toys that might give your puppy the wrong idea – for example, toys that look like shoes are very likely to give your puppy the idea that it's OK to chew your shoes as well.

4. Beware toys or chews that are too desirable, particularly if your dog is prone to guarding behaviour – rawhide chews, for example, can be so well loved by puppies that they lead to possessive guarding behaviours.

As well as considering the toy or chew itself, it's also worth considering the influence you may have through the way in which you use the toy and interact with your dog. One of the common mistakes owners make which can lead to further behavioural problems is to try to remove a toy or chew from a puppy's mouth by force. This approach risks initiating aggressive behaviours, not to mention the potential for causing physical injury to the puppy (and you). It is always much better to use distraction or reward techniques if you want your puppy to let go of a particular toy or chew – so tempt him with a food treat and pick up the toy when he drops it to eat the treat. In this way you are taking the toy with no conflict, and rewarding him for dropping it in the process.

In cases where inappropriate destructive behaviours have become a problem, there are some relatively straightforward approaches that can often resolve things. By far and away the simplest and most effective technique is to use a novel or particularly interesting stimulus such as a squeaky toy to distract the puppy from the inappropriate behaviour. Clicker training can also work well in these situations by reinforcing the effect of a pleasant stimulus such as the squeaker toy.

The final point of discussion on inappropriate destructive behaviour in puppies is the use of negative training methods including deterrent sounds and punishments. As we've already ascertained, punishments tend not to be either effective or productive in the long term when training dogs as all they achieve is to build up negative associations and fears, both of which can compound rather than cure behavioural problems. Deterrent sounds on the other hand can be useful, and the simplest form is a loud clap or sharp word in a firm tone of voice. This is usually sufficient to deter most puppies from whatever they are engaged in and, if followed by some positive distracting behaviour, is usually an effective way of stopping the behaviour. If clapping or shouting is not effective, some people recommend the use of a shaker can to startle the puppy and deter them from the behaviour. This can simply be a plastic drink bottle or tin can with a few stones inside that you shake loudly near the puppy if you want to deter them from whatever they are doing, or, if you want to be more sophisticated, you can try combining a specific smell with the noise of the shaker can. The idea here is to build up an association in the puppy's mind between the negative feelings the noise of the shaker can elicits and a particular smell – for example lemon or citronella. By making the shaker can smell of citronella, you can then use the smell alone to act as a deterrent on things that you don't want the puppy to chew, such as electrical wires.

Joe's TV Casebook

ELECTRIC-SHOCK COLLARS ON *THE ONE SHOW*

The use of electric-shock collars to prevent inappropriate behaviours in dogs, such as chasing livestock or other dogs, is a very contentious issue, as I found out on a reporting assignment for *The One Show* on BBC 1. The story revolved around the news that the Welsh Assembly had decided to ban the use of these collars in Wales because of a report that showed conclusively that these collars caused stress to dogs. I was sent off to interview a dog owner who felt that these collars were very effective and had saved her dog from having to be put down due to his behavioural problem of running away and chasing sheep. Putting forward the anti-electric-collar viewpoint was respected dog trainer Sarah Fisher, who condemned the collars as barbaric and showed how more positive and humane techniques including clicker training could provide an effective alternative, even in extreme cases involving dogs worrying sheep.

It was a lively debate and, although I had my own clear views on the subject (I think devices like this are abominable and have no place in dog training), I had to try to remain as impartial as I could and let both parties put forward their views.

However, my impartiality was tested to the limit when I volunteered to try out one of these collars myself and I experienced firsthand the true brutality of the electric shock these devices deliver. It was really unpleasant, and I only felt it on my hand not my neck, so I can only guess how painful it must be for the dogs who have to wear these devices.

It was an interesting film to make, and hopefully one that made dog owners think carefully about how powerful these collars can be and, thanks to Sarah's input, how unnecessary they are when there are so many better, safer training techniques available.

If you want to get really sophisticated, for a particularly stubborn inappropriate behaviour, you can consider setting up safe but scary booby traps which provide a shock at the exact time the behaviour is initiated. Examples include a shaker can balanced on a shelf and attached by a thin thread to the item you want the dog to leave alone, such as a shoe. If the puppy starts to chew or pull the shoe, the can will fall from the shelf making a loud and scary noise. Personally I wouldn't recommend this approach unless you've persisted with more positive methods, and probably also consulted a behavioural specialist, as I don't believe it's good for your overall relationship with your dog to be using such negative tactics.

The final type of inappropriate behaviour to consider is eating disorders. Now it might sound a bit funny to be discussing eating disorders in dogs, as I guess most people would think of this as a purely human issue. It's true that problems such as anorexia and bulimia are specific (as far as

I'm aware) to people, but there are also some very common and significant eating disorders that occur in dogs, namely scavenging and coprophagia.

Scavenging, or pica (a term used to describe eating non-food items), can be a real issue for some dogs, with complex causes including some medical conditions. Therefore, it's worth having your dog checked over physically by your vet if this is a serious issue for him. It could be that some underlying condition such as hypothyroidism or a malabsorption condition leaving him continually hungry is the main problem, rather than it being purely behavioural in nature.

If a scavenging habit or pica turns out to have no medical cause, then you need to consider the behavioural and psychological factors that have led to the problem if it is going to be solved. Some dogs scavenge because they are anxious, have compulsive tendencies or simply because they have a naturally large appetite, while others will do so out of hyperactive curiosity; there are many reasons and each case needs to be considered individually if it is going to be successfully treated. For example, a dog with a compulsive or anxiety-based scavenging habit will need a more subtle and careful approach than a dog whose only problem is controlling a large appetite or natural curiosity.

The basic tools at your disposal for tackling a scavenging habit are ones we have already covered in the discussions on inappropriate toilet activity and destructive behaviours – distraction with positive stimuli such as treats, and negative reinforcement using intimidating stimuli such as sounds and odours associated with sounds. Again, distraction is usually the best and kindest option to use, and is generally effective – the typical example would be offering a food treat to entice the dog to drop something less appropriate such as something scavenged from a bin. This is far better, and safer, than trying to forcibly remove an object from your dog's mouth, and has the secondary benefit of rewarding the action of dropping the inappropriate object. If you combine the treat with a command such as 'Drop it!' you should find that in time your dog will become conditioned to the command and no longer need the treat.

Negative reinforcement techniques such as those used to prevent inappropriate destructive behaviours in the house can be useful, particularly in cases where more positive techniques have been tried and have not succeeded, but again I would urge caution. It is all too easy to see a negative deterrent as an easy option, but, in nine cases out of ten, the positive approach is just as or more effective and has a much better long-term effect on your relationship with your dog.

Coprophagia (eating faeces) is one of the least endearing habits of many dogs and is often one of the harder inappropriate behavioural problems to deal with. The reasons behind coprophagia are often complex and involve a combination of behavioural, dietary and environmental factors, so getting to the bottom (no pun intended!) of the problem is often very hard to do. This makes finding an effective solution much more challenging.

One of the most commonly suggested theories as to why

dogs eat faeces is a territorial behaviour issue; dogs eat the faeces of other dogs in order to eliminate their territorial smells from the environment. If, like me, you find this theory hard to swallow (again, no pun intended!), then I think you're probably right. I cannot see this being a realistic reason for eating faeces, and, while it may be a very minor contributing factor in a small number of cases, I think there are almost certainly more convincing reasons behind this problem. Instead, I feel that, if there is a behavioural issue, it's more likely to be relevant in dogs that eat their own faeces rather than those of other dogs, and is based on a fear of inappropriate defecation. Dogs that have been house trained using negative training methods may well develop fears and anxieties associated with going to the toilet, as we discussed previously, and one reaction to this is to gobble up their faeces as soon as they have been passed in an attempt to hide the evidence.

Aside from behavioural factors, I also believe that diet plays a large role, as many coprophagic dogs are also scavengers, and eating faeces can be an extension of this trait if the faeces contain some residual nutrients. This tends to happen if the dog is being fed on a low-quality diet which is poorly digestible, leading to faeces containing relatively high levels of residual protein and carbohydrate. Dogs, with their acute sense of smell, can easily detect these trace levels of nutrients in faeces, and, if they are desperately hungry or compulsive scavengers, then their desire for food will overcome any inherent distaste for eating faeces.

Whatever the cause of a coprophagia problem, there are a

few recognised and generally effective techniques for curing the problem:

- Remove temptation – pick up your dog's faeces and any other faeces that he may come into contact with before he gets a chance to eat them.

- Prevent access – if your dog is a habitual eater of other dogs' faeces while out on walks, try a basket muzzle to physically prevent him from being able to eat poo.

- Deterrents – the idea of making a dog's faeces taste so bad to him that he won't eat them is as old as the problem of coprophagia in domestic dogs, with lots of things from chillies to mints having been tried to remedy this problem. In my experience, however, few of them are effective. Having said that, there are some products on the market which do occasionally work, so it's worth a try if you're at your wit's end with this problem – but just don't expect miracles!

- Change diet – this is probably the most effective approach, as diet is thought to play a significant role in many coprophagia cases. If you are feeding a low-quality complete food, then upgrade to a better-quality one as this should reduce the amount of faeces and the amount of residual nutrients in the faeces, and you can also try adding extra fibre, such as grated vegetables, to alter the texture of the faeces. One other approach suggested by various vets is to feed a high-protein/low-carbohydrate diet supplemented with additional vegetable oil, but this is not something I've ever had experience of so I can't comment on how effective or not it might be.

FEARS AND PHOBIAS

Fear can be a major problem for many dogs and their owners, and drive a number of behavioural problems, including some forms of aggression, separation anxiety and specific phobias such as fear of fireworks or thunder. It often appears to be a very difficult problem to solve, as the more effort you put into reassuring your dog and trying to help them cope with the fear-inducing stimuli, the worse the problem seems to get. But if we place the fear in the context of the dog's environment and relationships, and apply some rational behaviour theory to the problem, we can usually find a solution to most fear-related behavioural problems.

Before moving on to some of the specific problems such as separation anxiety, it's worth understanding the various ways in which dogs react to fearful stimuli. These can be summarised by the five 'F's of fear:

1. Flee – run away from the fear-inducing stimulus
2. Fight – channel fear into aggression or another inappropriate behaviour (attack is the best form of defence, as the old saying goes)
3. Freeze – paws over the eyes and wait for the stimulus to end
4. Flirt – cautiously investigate the stimulus while maintaining vigilance
5. Forbear – put up with the situation and get on with things

Obviously, dogs with fear-related problems tend to react in

one of the first ways described above. The goal of treatment of these problems is to move their response down the list, so a dog that flees or fights may be reconditioned to freeze or flirt or even forbear.

The basic techniques available for managing fear problems are confidence building and counter-conditioning. Confidence building is exactly what it sounds like – gradually helping your dog to be more confident and less fearful when confronted by the fear-inducing stimulus, whereas counter-conditioning is a slightly more technical method which we will look at in some detail.

There are a range of fear-induced problems that dogs suffer from, with similar causes and treatments, so, rather than going through each one individually, I will identify the most common and serious example in some detail. Everything that is mentioned in this example also applies to other fear issues. It's just a case of taking the principles and applying them to your dog's particular circumstances.

Separation anxiety is a term used to describe serious and debilitating stress caused by separation or isolation from key family members. Typical manifestations of separation anxiety include dogs that bark all day when left alone, or engage in destructive or inappropriate behaviours such as chewing, biting or urination and defecation in the house. Needless to say, the results of this kind of behaviour problem can be very unpleasant. I have come across many cases over the years that have become so serious that they have led to a total breakdown in the relationship between dog and owner and even in a few cases to the owner asking to have their dog destroyed because they could no longer cope. Thankfully most cases of separation anxiety are nowhere nearly as severe, but it does go to show just how serious they can be – and the vital importance of taking early action if your dog starts to show any signs at all of suffering from this, or any other form of fear problem.

As with most behavioural problems, separation anxiety is primarily an owner – rather than a dog – problem. Apart from those very rare exceptions where the temperament and character of the dog is a major contributing factor, most fear problems come down to the way your dog interacts with you. It may well be unconscious on your part, but subtle cues, such as over-reacting to potentially fearful stimuli such as another dog barking, or over-reassurance which reinforces fearful associations and fearful body language, play a major role in the development of fear problems such as separation anxiety. Separation anxiety does not occur in wild dogs, at least not to the same clinically significant degree as it does in domestic animals, so there is no doubt that we are the authors of this problem. The answer to the problem usually lies largely with us, not our dogs.

In the case of separation anxiety, let's go back to our typical dog-owning family, the Smiths and their dog Rover, to illustrate how such a problem could develop. Rover is often left on his own for long periods in the day while Mr and Mrs Smith are both at work. To begin with, this was of little concern to Rover as he was quite content lying in his bed day dreaming about the long walk that evening. However, it worried Rover's owners, and Mrs Smith in particular, who was increasingly concerned about the effect being left alone for such a long period each day was having on the dog. To try to compensate, she made sure she gave him loads of attention just before she left for work, and then again when she came home, giving him a big cuddle as soon as he ran up to her when she opened the door. She also began to relax the house rules and let Rover up on to the sofa and occasionally allowed him to sleep at the foot of their bed. This all helped Mrs Smith feel slightly less guilty – but sadly the effect on Rover was very different. Previously he'd been quite content, knowing his place at the bottom of the family social hierarchy, and secure in the knowledge that his owners would return home at some point whenever they went out. But now, with the extra attention he was getting just before they left for work and as soon as they got home, he started to feel anxious when they left – if they were worried, then there must be something to worry about, he thought subconsciously. These fears gradually began to increase as the weeks went by, reinforced by Mrs Smith's increasingly enthusiastic attentions, especially when she got home. In Rover's mind, all this attention could only mean one thing – there must be something to worry about when they go out, or they wouldn't be so excited to be home again. Add to this his increasing dependence on Mrs Smith brought about by the new relaxed house rules, and you can start to see how confused and stressed he became.

It might sound a bit much to be theorising about a dog

making these connections and having these thoughts, but I'm not suggesting that these are real conscious thoughts – I'm just trying to illustrate the subconscious process that is going on in response to the actions of the owner deep in Rover's mind, and how it affects his behaviour.

With Mrs Smith becoming more and more worried and over-compensating with extra attention when she leaves and returns home, Rover is starting to increasingly associate her leaving the house with stress, worry and fear. As we've seen, there are various ways in which he can react to this fear – the five 'F's. In his case, he can't flee the fear, so instead he reacts by fighting. This is not literal fighting, but a term I've used to describe displacement behaviour which can include aggression. In Rover's case, there is nothing to fight, so instead he takes his fear out on whatever he can find – the sofa, Mr Smith's shoes, the skirting boards and anything else he can chew and destroy.

Once this behaviour starts, the reaction of the Smiths is typical – they are upset and angry with Rover, and punish him when they get home, making a great fuss about what has happened. Rover is confused and stressed by this response, and he becomes even more fearful – his owners' reaction has simply reinforced his subconscious association between their leaving the house and bad things happening. Things go from bad to worse, and within a few short months the Smiths are at their wits' end with a house in pieces and Rover is confined to the kitchen where, with nothing to chew, he expresses his fear by howling all day long.

I hope this illustrates one way in which the owner creates and then fuels a dog's fear, and how the dog is usually an innocent party. In Rover's case, he was responsible for chewing the shoes and ripping up the sofa, but the reason he felt compelled to do this was based on a fear that had been created by the anxiety of his owners and reinforced by their reactions to his initial actions.

Before we look at how to cure separation anxiety using confidence building and counter-conditioning, it's important to emphasise the importance of prevention in these cases. It's all too easy to react as the Smiths did in my example and figuratively pour petrol on a smouldering fire that would be relatively easy to extinguish early on. The most important factors to remember if you are faced with a dog showing the early signs of a fear-induced behavioural problem are:

- Don't fuel his anxieties – Remember, your dog will look to you and observe your reaction, so, if you get excited or show signs of anxiety yourself in response to your dog's fears, these will simply serve to confirm to your dog that there is something to be scared of.

- Be careful what you punish – When faced with a dog who has clearly done something inappropriate such as chew your shoes, don't make the mistake of punishing him when you find out, because it will almost certainly be too late and your dog will associate the negative emotions of being punished with you rather than whatever action it was he took, thus failing to have any effect on his errant behaviour and serving only to damage your relationship with him.

•Be even more careful what you reward – Over-indulging your dog with attention can do more harm than good, especially in the case of separation anxiety where your well-meaning reward response to coming home and seeing your dog can be a major factor in inducing over-attachment and therefore contribute to separation anxiety.

In conventional cases of separation anxiety, there are two well-established techniques for resolving the problem – confidence building and counter-conditioning – as well as a third approach of resolving any underlying relationship issues.

Fear is usually associated with a lack of confidence – a dog who is scared of thunder loses confidence in their ability to cope if they hear thunder; a dog with separation anxiety loses confidence that they can cope without their owner present and so on – so restoring and rebuilding this confidence is an important factor in dealing with fear-induced behavioural problems. In the case of separation anxiety, this is a gradual process (which usually runs alongside the process of counter-conditioning) in which the dog learns that they can survive without their owners, that nothing terrible will happen when alone, and that their fears are unfounded. Achieving this in practice is not always as easy as it sounds, and there is always the inherent risk of veering into inappropriate reward or reinforcement behaviour where confidence building becomes reassurance. This may sound the same but is crucially different. Reassurance comes from you rather than from the dog himself, and therefore is effective when you are present. If your dog is relying on your reassurance as a crutch, when you're not present he is even worse off than before. Remember that dogs are comparatively simple animals and cannot easily link feelings and emotions across time periods, so you reassuring your dog that it'll all be allright when you are there will provide reassurance and contentment at that moment in time – but, as soon as you leave, the positive feelings of reassurance leave with you and your dog is left as fearful as before. Confidence, on the other hand, comes from within. While you may be instrumental in building that confidence, it is a quality your dog owns and can rely on even when you are not present. Building confidence is about empowering your dog to cope on their own, whereas reassurance is simply a short-term solution that treats rather than cures symptoms.

The trick to confidence building is to allow your dog to experience the fearful situation or stimulus in such a way that he feels safe. This can be achieved by distraction (which is also one of the key elements of counter-conditioning which we will come on to next) and by modifying the environment to minimise the impact of the stimulus. Examples of this approach include keeping doors, windows and curtains closed during fireworks displays to minimise the noise and light that scare the dog, or playing a recording of your voice in an adjacent room when leaving your dog to fool them into believing you are still present when you're not.

Counter-conditioning is a powerful behavioural tool that uses the theory of classical conditioning outlined previously to rebuild subconscious associations in the mind, replacing negative links with positive ones. An example of this approach would be in the case of a dog who is fearful of strangers. The problem is a conditioned association between a stranger and the emotion of fear, possibly caused by previous negative experiences with intimidating strangers. As soon as the dog sees a stranger, he feels scared, and no amount of coercing or reassurance is going to change that inbuilt association. The process of counter-conditioning, however, can undo that negative link and replace it with a positive one so that eventually the dog begins to associate strangers with positive emotions rather than fear. Practically this is achieved by getting strangers to offer the dog rewards such as food while behaving in as non-threatening a manner as possible. What should happen is that the desire for the reward overcomes the fear, and gradually the conditioned link between stranger and fear is broken down and replaced by a new one between stranger and food.

In the case of separation anxiety, the link that needs to be counter-conditioned is between your absence and emotions of fear, anxiety and stress. The underlying cause of the problem is usually the dog's over-dependence on you. The only way to effectively remove the separation anxiety is to initially address any imbalances in the fundamentals of your relationship with your dog – often easier said than done. The main imbalance that leads to separation anxiety is an overly dependent bond between your dog and you which leaves your dog feeling fearful and anxious when you are not present. Addressing this issue is just as important as the counter-conditioning process itself, and involves making some tough decisions about the way you live your life with your dog.

Before we get on to the specifics of how we address relationship issues underlying separation anxiety, let's consider the main process of counter-conditioning. This is usually achieved by a gradual process of desensitisation in which the association between your absence and the associated negative feelings is dismantled, to be replaced by a feeling of calm and relaxation. In practice, this involves implementing a regime whereby you gradually remove any stressful connotations linked to your leaving, as well as the positive ones linked to your returning (as they are just as important), and allow your dog to build new associations between being alone and the relaxed feelings you have allowed him to feel – which are incompatible with fear.

The easiest way to explain a practical approach to dealing with a situation where counter-conditioning, confidence building and correcting underlying relationship issues are combined is to set out the kind of typical 'treatment' regime that I have found to be successful in cases I've dealt with in the surgery:

STEP 1: REBUILD YOUR RELATIONSHIP

Over-dependence, which is the basis of most cases of separation anxiety, is usually caused by poor discipline and a misunderstanding of the dog's place in the family pack, both by you and the dog. Over-dependent dogs tend to be over-indulged with attention and unrestricted by ground rules governing their behaviour – in short, they're spoiled. This overly close bond without the usual clear sense of differentiation between dog and master predisposes these dogs to separation anxiety, and breaking down this bond is key to resolving the problem.

This doesn't mean you suddenly have to be unpleasant to your dog, or that he will love you any less – it's about replacing an overly-close bond with a normal, happy bond that frees both of you from the pressures and consequences of over-dependence. This is achieved by setting down clear house rules and sticking to them. Rules will vary depending on your circumstances, but, as discussed in Chapter Two, they need to cover the main areas of your dog's life including where they can and can't go in the house, where and when they are fed, and where they sleep.

In addition to setting out ground rules preventing the dog from jumping up on the sofa and so on, it is also important to eliminate any behavioural patterns at home that could also be contributing to this over-dependence, such as the dog initiating play activities and demanding (and getting) attention. Remember, as the leader of the pack, you, the owner, call the shots.

With these relationship basics in place, it's then time to move on to step two to start the confidence-building and counter-conditioning processes.

STEP 2: REDUCE THE STRESS

In most cases of separation anxiety, the dog's fears are fuelled by the actions of an overly concerned owner (such as our Mrs

Smith) who works the dog up into a state of stress before leaving the house. Reducing this stressful stimulation prior to departure is crucial and is the first step in the counter-conditioning and confidence-building processes.

To achieve this, you need to set in place the following strict rules for whenever you leave home:

1. Stop any interaction with your dog one hour before you leave the house.
2. Twenty minutes before you leave, put the dog in the room that they will be in while you're out.
3. When you are ready to leave, wait for 10–15 minutes in another room before actually leaving the house. This takes away the link between the dog being shut away and your actually leaving, so the act of being shut away is not so stressful and doesn't immediately lead to an anxiety attack.
4. Upon your return, ignore the dog completely, leaving him where he is, and wait 10 minutes, or until he is calm (whichever is longer), before paying him any attention.

You can also help with the confidence-building side of the solution by leaving a recording of your voice playing elsewhere in the house, or giving your dog a special toy to play with while you are out.

The rules I've outlined above are for the most serious cases and are not always applicable in less severe instances. It pays to remember the principles of the rules so, if you're faced with a milder case of separation anxiety, you can put in place a less strict version.

STEP 3: COUNTER-CONDITIONING

With the stress of departure and return reduced, you can start to retrain your dog's subconscious to remove his stressful associations. This is achieved through a process of desensitisation and reconditioning, whereby you gradually expose your dog to longer and longer periods of isolation while managing the emotions he feels during your absence. As he spends more and more time alone not feeling fearful, but relaxed and happy instead, he will slowly become reconditioned to associate being alone with positive feelings rather than negative ones. Practically, this is achieved as follows:

1. The dog is exposed to very short periods of isolation, preceded by the calm, stress-free approach outlined in the second step. This isolation may initially be simply putting the dog in another room rather than involving your actually leaving the house, but, however it is achieved, you should focus on your dog remaining calm and happy throughout the period of isolation. This is best achieved through distraction with a positive stimulus – giving him a new and interesting toy, or food to find in the room, for example. Feeding toys, where pieces of food can be inserted into a toy, are particularly useful here as they can keep a dog distracted and happy for long periods of time. Make sure you end the

isolation well before the distraction wears off, and, when you do so, make no fuss whatsoever – just let the dog out as if nothing out of the ordinary has happened and ignore him if he is excited.

2. Gradually extend these periods of isolation and the degree of isolation until your dog is happy being left completely alone for an hour or more. This process needs to be carefully managed to make sure that at no point does your dog show any signs of stress or fear. This may mean that the process could take many weeks.

3. Complete the counter-conditioning by removing any stress or fear related to pre-departure cues such as picking up keys or putting on a coat. This is achieved by doing these actions but not actually leaving the house – so do everything you might normally do before you leave, but then stay put without going out. Again, it's vital that you remain calm and don't give your dog any attention whatsoever before or after your mock departure – remember that you are trying to teach your dog that there is nothing interesting or exciting about your leaving the house.

This regime should, if followed strictly, be all you need to resolve your dog's separation anxiety. Never forget, though, that all the counter-conditioning and confidence building in the world won't be effective if there's a flaw in your basic relationship with your dog such as over-dependence. As with most aspects of living with our dogs, it's not the dog that's the problem, it's the owner – and we can prove much harder to change than our pets!

COMPULSIONS AND HYPERACTIVITY

There's a little bit of the obsessive-compulsive in all of us say the human psychologists. To some degree, the same can be said about our canine companions. Clinical compulsive disorders such as tail biting, excessive licking, chasing shadows and so on might be relatively uncommon, but just as with people there's a spectrum from a minor tendency right up to a full-blown clinical disorder. So understanding how these disorders arise, and how to cope with them, is important not just for those of us with dogs exhibiting the more serious syndromes, but for all dog owners trying to appreciate every mental current that make our dogs behave the way they do.

Like most behaviour problems, compulsive and hyperactivity disorders in dogs involve disturbances or exaggerations of normal behaviour patterns – so the dog that spends his days barking for attention or pacing or licking is simply doing a normal action in a pathologically abnormal manner. It might sound a bit over the top to describe something such as tail biting as a pathological condition, but, in reality, any disorder that leads to negative consequences could be defined as pathological in the strict sense of the word. Don't be fooled by these conditions – despite sometimes appearing humorous or inconsequential, in most cases dogs that are exhibiting this kind of abnormal behaviour are doing so as a way of expressing frustration and depression and there is nothing funny about them from their point of view.

Before looking at the causes of compulsive and hyperactive disorders, I'll quickly run through some of the more common examples and manifestations of these problems in dogs:

- Tail biting – It's not uncommon for a dog to occasionally bite their tail, but some dogs do so in an obsessive manner which can lead to serious physical injuries caused by self-mutilation as well as the psychological issues the behaviour expresses.
- Shadow chasing and air biting – Relatively common in some breeds of Spaniel, this is one of those conditions that sound amusing but is in reality no fun for dog or owner after a while.
- Attention seeking – Dogs who constantly push their noses into your lap or bark incessantly in order to attract your attention.
- Physical excessive behaviours – Pacing, jumping up and down and carpet digging are all examples of compulsive disorders.
- Sexual behaviours – The classic issue of dogs humping the leg of a visitor to the house might sound amusing, but for the dog it can represent a serious underlying issue.

Most of these disorders arise from the excessive expression of a normal behaviour, whether it be grooming (in the case of tail biting), social interaction (attention seeking) or sexual behaviours. The reasons why these behaviours become exaggerated and abnormal are complex, but there are some general underlying issues that often contribute to the development of this kind of disorder:

- Frustration – Dogs confined to an excessively small area such as a crate or small room can become seriously frustrated. This can lead directly to the development of compulsive behaviours such as pacing or barking. Another term for this type of reaction to frustrating circumstances is a stereotypic behaviour and is seen in all species of domestic or confined animals, from horses biting their stable doors to lions pacing up and down in their zoo cages hour after hour.

- Excitement – Compulsive and hyperactive disorders are often displayed during times of excitement, which suggests that this kind of behavioural excess serves as a release for pent-up energy and excitement.

- Genetics – There is a proven genetic link to this type of disorder in dogs, with certain breeds and types of dogs being much more prone to specific problems than others. Within a breed or group, it is often highly strung individuals that are the worst affected, which fits in with the idea that these behaviours are driven by pent-up energy and frustration.

- Diet – The idea that artificial additives such as tartrazine, which are commonly found in many pet foods and have been linked with hyperactivity in children, may contribute to behavioural problems in dogs has gained acceptance during the last few years. Anecdotal evidence from my own clients and from dog trainers I have talked

to leaves me in little doubt that diet can play a role in behavioural disorders, particularly those involving compulsions and hyperactivity. As well as artificial additives, there is also thought to be a link between protein levels in food and hyperactivity. This has been less clearly established, although there is some theoretical reasoning behind the idea that low-protein, high-carbohydrate diets appear to facilitate the uptake of tryptophan into the brain. Tryptophan is a precursor of a molecule called 5-HT which plays an important role in controlling obsessive compulsive behaviours, so there may well be something in this idea.

Treating severe compulsive and hyperactivity disorders is really a subject for a clinical behaviourist who is better equipped to deal with the harder and more complex behavioural problems. Having said that, in cases at the milder end of the clinical spectrum there are certainly things that you can do yourself to try to rectify the problem before it becomes a full-blown disorder.

The most obvious thing to do is to remove any causal factors that might be contributing to the development of the behaviour, such as the excessive periods of confinement leading to frustration and episodes of over-excitement that can trigger compulsive actions. It's also well worth looking at the diet your dog is receiving. If they are being fed a high-protein food or one with artificial additives, consider trying a lower-protein natural alternative.

Joe's Behaviour Casebook

THEY ARE WHAT THEY EAT!

'I can tell exactly what kind of diet a dog eats as soon as they walk through the door,' an experienced dog trainer and behaviourist told me as we chatted about the role of diet in dog behaviour. 'If they're fed on a cheap diet with lots of artificial nasties, they come in bouncing off the walls and they're a nightmare to train.'

Her experience confirmed my own views on the important role that diet plays in canine behaviour. I'd also seen a similar link between the behaviour of dogs in my surgery and the diet they were being fed at home which led directly to my decision to set up my own pet-food company. Pets' Kitchen is all about making top-quality, 100 per cent natural food (free from artificial colours, preservatives and flavours) for dogs and cats based on my veterinary knowledge and home-cooking recipes, with a particular focus on making sure the foods are not only hypoallergenic to minimise allergies and intolerances wherever possible, but also completely free of the artificial additives I know were playing a large role in damaging the behaviour of many dogs.

The results have definitely borne out the hypothesis that food plays an important role in behaviour, with much anecdotal evidence coming from dog owners feeding our foods, and others like them, suggesting they really do make a big difference to dogs' behaviour, and in particular cases involving compulsive and hyperactivity problems.

Once any likely causal and contributing factors are addressed, you can think about more direct measures to try to help your dog out of the mental state that is leading to these compulsions or excesses. But before you do so it's worth emphasising that there is no point targeting the behaviour unless you address the underlying factors, as the behaviour itself is only the tip of the iceberg. The worst thing you can do is to physically prevent your dog from expressing the behaviour, misunderstanding it and neglecting the motivation behind it, as this will just lead to further frustration and stress. You may well succeed in preventing a specific behaviour by making it impossible or very undesirable for the dog to do it (for example, using an electric-shock collar to prevent excessive barking, or putting a lampshade collar on a dog to stop him biting his tail), but you won't have cured the problem. It's more than likely that the internal frustration will boil up again and find release in another compulsive behaviour – or simply leave your dog thoroughly miserable.

There are a couple of strategies you can employ to reduce or stop compulsive or hyperactive behaviours. The simplest approach is distraction. This is often reasonably effective, at least in the less severe cases. All that's required is to try to snap your dog out of his obsessive behaviour using a novel or particularly attractive distraction stimulus such as a food treat or squeaker toy.

If distraction isn't effective, or provides only a short-lived respite from the behaviour, you could consider trying a deterrent approach as the next step – although I would caution once again that it is imperative that the underlying causes behind the behaviour have been addressed before considering using negative techniques such as deterrents. If you do decide to try a deterrent, there are many options available, ranging from the simple verbal command in a stern tone of voice to a shaker tin or modern electronic devices such as scent-releasing collars for barking (although personally I would be very wary of resorting to anything like this without first consulting a properly qualified behaviourist).

The final approach to mention might initially sound counter-intuitive, but it can work remarkably well for certain dogs. This approach is called stimulus control and involves your bringing the behaviour under your control by conditioning your dog to link the behaviour with a command (or click if you use clicker training, etc). Once this association has been made, you are in a position to use your normal training methods to exert control over the behaviour because your dog will theoretically only undertake the behaviour if and when they hear the command you have associated with it, and they will also stop it when you issue your normal stop command. Unfortunately, this approach is not usually quite as straightforward as it sounds, and is something usually best attempted under the guidance of a behaviourist.

AGGRESSION

The behavioural issues we've considered to this point have all been problems capable of causing significant distress to dog and family alike, but not actual physical harm. As we turn our attention to the most serious behavioural problems, those involving aggression, however, we are confronting a spectrum of behavioural disorders that have the potential to cause injury and even death not just to other dogs but also to people. Most of us, I'm sure, can recall shocking stories of children being savaged by aggressive dogs, and probably also have personal experiences of meeting intimidating dogs or even being attacked by one, so aggression problems are both relatively common, and also high profile.

Aggression is the ultimate example of a relationship gone wrong. Dogs have evolved to avoid physical conflict at all costs, using the rigid social hierarchy of the pack system to remove the need for serious conflicts in social disputes, so, when they turn to this form of behaviour, it is a sign that something serious is wrong with them or their social environment. Dogs that attack other dogs may do so out of an exaggerated sense of fear driven by poor socialisation. Dogs that attack people often do so because of confusion in the social order within their family environment. Dogs that suddenly turn from passive to aggressive may be reacting to deep internal frustrations for which aggression is the only release they can find.

There are many ways to classify aggression, using complex systems of neurophysiology and behavioural theories, but personally I think it is easier to think of the causes of canine aggression as falling into two broad groups – fear-driven and dominance-driven.

Fear-aggression is, as the name suggests, the embodiment of the 'attack is the best form of defence' school of thought. As we've already seen, fear is a significant emotion in dogs and drives many forms of abnormal behaviour including anxiety and disobedience. However, the most significant behavioural problem produced by deep-seated fear is defensive aggression and this can lead to some of the worst cases of dog versus dog and dog versus human aggression.

The way in which fear triggers aggression in dogs is relatively simple – as we've already seen with the five 'F's of fear, dogs are limited in how they can respond to fearful stimuli, and, when circumstance further reduces their options, they are often left with fight as the only path to take. A typical example would be a dog that is perfectly well mannered with other dogs when off the lead, but who turns into a snarling nightmare when he meets other dogs when he is on the lead (my dog Jack is a good example of this!). Being on the lead immediately takes away his number-one preferred option of 'flee' when faced with a fear-inducing stimulus. Another classic example is one that is particularly relevant to my profession – perfectly good-natured dogs who turn into vet-attacking beasts as soon as they are dragged into the consulting room. Again, it's all down to fear and the removal of escape routes leaving the dog with no option but to externalise their fear through aggression. The only consolation for the vet about to have his fingers bitten off is that the dog is almost certainly more scared than he is!

Prevention is by far and away the best approach to fear-aggression and a properly raised and well-socialised dog is very unlikely to be at risk of developing this problem. The main contributing factors, apart from inherent genetic ones such as a nervous temperament or inclination towards aggression, all relate to puppyhood – not learning how to interact with other dogs at a young age; over-protective owner during puppyhood; bad experiences (such as being attacked by another dog) during formative months; neglect or abuse. Ensuring you bring your puppy up in a safe, secure and harmonious social environment, with plenty of time for socialisation and interaction with other dogs and children in particular, is the best way by far to prevent fear-aggression problems later in life.

If fear-aggression does occur, or perhaps you inherit a dog with such a problem (as I did with Jack), then there are various measures you can use to try to reduce the severity of the problem and the risks to you, your family and other dogs. Obviously if the problem is severe then you need professional help from a behaviourist, but for those cases where the problem is relatively mild and intermittent, you can certainly try to resolve matters yourself.

- Avoidance – The first step to take is to reduce the chances of an aggressive episode occurring by reducing your dog's exposure to situations that trigger his aggression. This might mean finding a quiet field to walk him in to avoid other dogs, or keeping the dog away from children depending on his particular fear.
- Distraction – This is a technique that I have used to great effect with Jack when he gets funny with other dogs and has really helped me cope with his problem. All you need to do is distract your dog with a treat or toy whenever you are aware that he might be becoming scared and potentially aggressive. With a bit of luck you'll be able to circumvent the situation with your dog's attention

focused on the treat, and, by the time he realises what's happened, the fearful stimulus will have gone.

- Counter-conditioning – Just as for cases of separation anxiety (also driven by fear), it is possible to retrain your dog's mind so that he no longer associates the fear-inducing stimulus with the emotion of fear and instead links it with positive emotion or feeling such as that linked to food. The typical example is that of a dog who is scared of and aggressive towards strangers. By your asking strangers to give the dog treats, the fear can gradually be replaced by reward.
- Confidence building – Again, as with separation anxiety, confidence building goes hand in hand with counter-conditioning. Gradually getting your dog used to the fear-inducing stimulus through repeated low-level exposure can help reduce his fear levels significantly.

These four strategies can work wonders for fear-aggressive dogs (they certainly did for Jack), but there are also some equally powerful pitfalls that you must avoid if you are to resolve this kind of problem:

- Over-reassurance – It's all very well giving your dog confidence-building reassurance when they are faced with their greatest fear, but you must be careful not to actually do the opposite and reduce their confidence by increasing their reliance on you in stressful situations. Not only will this make them less self-confident, it could also contribute to other behavioural problems, including separation anxiety, which is often driven by over-reassurance and over-dependence.

• Showing fear – Your dog looks to you, as leader of his pack, for guidance when faced with a stressful or fearful situation, so, if he turns round to see his owner quivering like a leaf at the sight of a large dog coming your way, this is not going to fill him with confidence. It's important that, even if you do find the situation scary, you must do your best not to let your dog know this. Put on a brave face, stiff upper lip and all that, and act like a fearless leader even if you are quivering inside!

The extension of this theory suggests that, far from showing fear or nervousness in the face of a scary situation such as the approach of a large dog, you, as leader of the pack, should be the first one to launch the attack. According to this reasoning, your dog displays aggression to protect you from the situation he perceives as scary, and, by getting in first with a loud growl and aggressive posture, he will feel protected and safe and no longer have the urge to attack himself.

It's an interesting theory and, while I can see the logic, and have witnessed it being successful in practice, it's not one I can wholeheartedly recommend unless you are absolutely happy with the idea of taking on a large, possibly angry dog on your own!

The second broad class of aggression is dominance-aggression. As the name suggests, this type of problem is directly linked to issues related to the dominance–submissive hierarchy underpinning the canine social world. The idea behind the pack social order is that it reduces conflict as every dog knows his place and therefore knows who to be subservient to and who he can boss around. Conflicts only tend to arise either when a dog tries to climb the social ladder by challenging dogs above him in the pecking order, or because there is confusion in the ranks – the prime cause of dominance-aggression problems in domestic dogs.

Dogs like order and they like to know where they stand. Confusion, particularly in relation to their position in the pack social structure, is not well tolerated and can become a prime factor in initiating aggression problems. This makes them insecure, and insecurity inevitably leads to conflict, which can either become internalised, and contribute to obsessive behavioural disorders, or externalised in the form of aggression. This aggression can be directed towards other dogs, but strangers and family members can also be recipients, which makes this kind of aggressive behaviour particularly dangerous and unpredictable.

Joe's Pets

JACK'S ISSUES

When I picked up my dog Jack from the Dog's Trust rescue centre in Evesham, Worcestershire, he seemed to be the most laid-back and well-behaved dog imaginable. However, it didn't take long before I realised that all was not quite as well as I'd thought.

The main issue I discovered was a classic case of fear-aggression. I'm lucky enough to live in the countryside where I can walk Jack off the lead most of the time. He was usually perfectly well behaved, coming when I called him and taking very little notice of any dogs we met along the way. Things changed, however, the very first time I put him on a lead for a walk – as soon as he spotted a dog coming towards us it was as if a switch had clicked inside his head and he turned into a growing, snapping, pulling nightmare, lunging on the lead to try to reach the poor innocent Labrador approaching.

After a few instances like this one, it became clear that Jack had a pretty bad case of fear-induced aggression directed towards other dogs. When he was off the lead, it was not a problem as he knew he could run away, but, as soon as he was on the lead, this option disappeared and left him with aggression as the only outlet for his fear.

Curing Jack of this problem has not been easy, as his fear was obviously deep rooted. I have no idea about his previous life before we took him on, but I think it's fairly clear that he didn't receive the correct level of socialisation as a puppy, and this has made changing his behaviour quite challenging.

The first approach I took was avoidance, so for the first few months we went for walks early in the morning and late at night and kept him off the lead where at all possible to minimise the chances of an encounter that might trigger an aggressive episode. And when we did come across another dog while Jack was on the lead I distracted him with a stick or ball, which proved to be very effective for him as he loves nothing more than his stick!

After stabilising the situation in this way, I gradually began to use some counter-conditioning tricks such as feeding him a

> treat while another dog walked past, and showed him by example that there was nothing to fear by meeting and greeting other dogs myself. I haven't yet had to resort to the owner-aggression tactic, but it's up my sleeve just in case things go wrong in the future!

As well as being influenced by social factors, genetic factors are also important in the development of dominance aggression. Some breeds are far more predisposed to this kind of behahiour – the classic guard-dog breeds such as Rottweillers, Dobermans and German Shepherds for example (not to say that the majority of these breeds aren't very well mannered before anyone takes offence – it's just that these breeds have an inherent tendency towards dominance and, if not correctly brought up, this makes them prone to aggressive tendencies). And then there are those breeds bred specifically for fighting, such as the Pit Bull Terrier, which have not so much a dominance problem but a simple genetic predisposition towards fighting created by centuries of selective breeding by people intent on creating fighting machines out of their dogs.

So there are many factors that play a role in the development of dominance–aggression problems. Nevertheless, there is still no reason for this problem to occur in the vast majority of dogs whatever their breed and genetic tendencies. Proper schooling and training and the establishment of a clear pack hierarchy within the household, with the dog at the bottom (or just above the cat!), should effectively prevent any problems with dominance aggression. This has been covered in detail in the chapter on puppyhood so I won't go into this again here, except to re-emphasise the need for clear ground rules and for you to have no doubt about your position of superiority and dominance over your dog.

Dealing with an existing dominance-aggression problem is really a job for the experts and will generally involve a multi-pronged approach using many of the techniques we have discussed in this chapter such as counter-conditioning, along with retraining programmes aimed at addressing the underlying issue of misplaced or confused dominance.

Before I leave the subject of behavioural issues, I would like to introduce one of the 'alternative' approaches to canine behaviour that I believe offers a viable option to more mainstream approaches, Tellington T-Touch.

The Tellington T-Touch is a kind and respectful way of working with dogs to help them overcome a variety of both health and behavioural issues which was developed over 30 years ago by Linda Tellington-Jones. It is now widely used around the world by trainers, shelter workers, vets, veterinary nurses and dog owners.

T-Touch recognises an inextricable link between posture and behaviour and uses body work, ground-work exercises and specific equipment to release tension and to promote a feeling of calm and wellbeing. This in turn helps dogs develop self-confidence and self-control and enables them to move beyond their instinctive and, often fearful, responses. This might sound a little new age for a science man like myself to believe in, but there is logic in this approach. For example, a dog that suffers from noise sensitivity or noise phobia is likely to carry tension through the hindquarters and tail and may dislike contact on or around his paws. His lower legs, tail and ears may also feel cold. The non-invasive body movements (T-Touches) can be used to improve circulation, thus warming up cold extremities, relax tight muscles and release habitual patterns of bracing. The movements can also induce calm and change the dog's expectation of what contact around his paws may mean. Stroking the ears helps to lower heart rate and respiration, while putting a body wrap or T-shirt on the dog can help to give a noise-sensitive dog a sense of security. As behaviours are usually linked, dogs with this pattern of tension through the body may also be nervous in new situations, be wary of strangers and find car travel difficult. T-Touch can help them to become more confident in all areas of their life without the need to address the individual concerns.

Contrary to the opinions of many behaviourists and trainers, T-Touch theory promotes the concept that handling a fearful, defensive or reactive animal in a positive, mindful, calm way does not reward, and therefore reinforce, negative behaviour. Indeed, it can change it. Advocates of the Tellington T-Touch believe it has a profound and potent effect on the nervous system and a powerful influence on responses and mood. Even well-established patterns of behaviour often alter within a very short space of time. It is an approach cited in saving the lives of many dogs whose behaviour has been deemed to be out of control.

As with all good behavioural practices, observations are an important part of T-Touch work. Practitioners note the dog's responses to stimuli, the posture, balance, movement and muscle development of the dog, his heart rate and respiration, the texture and appearance of the coat and so on. They feel for temperature changes, coarse or dry hair, tension in the tail, ears, legs and the mobility of the skin. They also pay close attention to the dog's responses to contact on the body and his ability to negotiate the ground-work exercises and adapt the sessions accordingly. The focus is always on what the dog can achieve rather than what he can't achieve with the aim to work below the threshold at which the dog has to react, particularly when handling animals that are nervous and/or defensive.

On a practical level, T-Touch involves body work and ground work. The body T-Touches break down into three groups: circles, slides and lifts. They consist of a variety of specific light-pressure touches and strokes which aim to increase mind/body awareness and to give the dog new information and experiences by engaging the sensory aspect of the nervous system. The circular T-Touches are the foundation of the T-Touch technique. The fingers or hand actually move the dog's skin gently in one and a quarter circles, usually in a clockwise direction, although some dogs prefer anti-clockwise circles – like a very gentle massage.

For the lifts, the hand gently lifts and supports the tissue of the body, then slowly releases it to the resting position. This often assists an animal to release muscle tension around a specific joint or body part and the lifts are usually used on legs, shoulders, hindquarters and along the back and neck.

The slides consist of slow gentle movements such as ear slides where the ear is stroked from the base right out to the tip, or long, mindful strokes that connect one body part to another. These reduce stress, reinforce the animal's spatial awareness and release tension.

The position of the hand and the pressure and type of T-Touch used will vary from dog to dog and will be dependent on the dog's responses to contact and the part of the body that is being touched. For example, nervous and defensive animals usually find contact with the back of the hand far less threatening and may initially only be able to tolerate being T-Touched on their shoulder.

The ground-work element of T-Touch involves leading dogs through patterns of poles laid on the ground, over low raised boards and see-saws and over different textures, which helps to improve proprioception (the brain's understanding of where the body is at any given time), focus and balance. The slow, precise movements of the ground-work exercises help dogs to settle and learn the ability to self-calm, and also increase flexibility and improve gait. Physical, emotional and mental balance are linked and the ground-work exercises can have a dramatic effect on behaviour and are particularly useful for dogs on reduced exercise or for those that become overly aroused when on the lead. They can also be a valuable starting point for dogs that cannot tolerate contact.

The Tellington-Touch helps to increase trust and

understanding between both the dog and his owner/carer. It benefits both the giver and the receiver and gives us a greater appreciation of our animal companions.

I am not generally a great believer in anything too alternative as all too often there is little science behind the hype, but with T-Touch I have seen firsthand the effectiveness of this approach, and also can see the similarities between the philosophy behind T-Touch and my own views in *Your Dog and You*. I was introduced to T-Touch by Sarah Fisher, an internationally respected animal trainer and T-Touch expert when we met filming an item on electric-shock collars for *The One Show*; I was really impressed by the way her approach seemed to work in a short period of time. We didn't agree on everything – she's not a proponent of the hierarchical school of dog training that I believe in – but we certainly did agree about the electric collars (cruel and unnecessary), and I left the shoot with a real enthusiasm for her gentle and compassionate approach to training and behaviour.

SEVEN

Health Problems

Having looked at the psychological and behavioural impacts of owner–dog relationship breakdown, in this chapter I'm going to consider those physical conditions where our relationship with our dog is of particular relevance. This is not a veterinary encyclopaedia – there are plenty of more comprehensive reference books available for that purpose – but instead a look at two specific health conditions that I believe are directly related to the way we live our lives with our dogs.

I may only be going to cover two problems, but they are two of the most common health issues affecting dogs, each presenting real challenges to treatment and prevention. Obesity is probably the number-one preventable health problem we see in dogs who attend surgery, and is entirely driven by the way the owner lives with the dog. The second condition is arthritis, and, while the underlying cause may not always be so specifically related to the actions of the owner, the way in which it is managed is very much a lifestyle issue.

OBESITY

Official figures from animal welfare organisations suggest that between a third and a half of all dogs are now either overweight or obese, and, from my personal experience in the surgery, I would suggest that these may even be conservative estimates. I estimate that well over half of the dogs that I see every day are overweight, with a significant proportion of these technically obese (this means they are more than 20 per cent above their ideal weight).

So obesity is clearly a significant issue, but how much actual clinical disease can we attribute to the growing waistlines of our dogs? There are some diseases where the impact of obesity is clear, such as arthritis where every extra pound a dog is carrying puts extra strain on the joints, or heart disease where extra effort is required to pump blood around the body, yet there are others where the link is less obvious, including diabetes, liver disease and some skin diseases. Put simply, obesity places an extra and unwelcome strain on the whole body and is a contributing factor in many clinical diseases. The end result is not just a reduced life expectancy brought about by these related clinical conditions, but, just as importantly, a reduced quality of life. Obese dogs are generally miserable dogs, unable to enjoy the basic pleasures that dogs should be able to take for granted – running, jumping, relaxing comfortably and so on. In most cases, they enter a vicious cycle of weight gain leading to reduced exercise and enjoyment which in turn leads to further weight gain and so on. Breaking this cycle is the key to treating an obese dog.

There are two main contributing factors to obesity in dogs, both directly related to their owners – too much food and not enough exercise. Dog owners always bring up other mitigating factors such as neutering or 'genetics', but at the end of the day these are only ever going to be minor effects that cannot cause the problem entirely by themselves – excessive consumption combined with inadequate exercise are by far and away the biggest factors and this should never be forgotten. It's all too easy for dog owners to put the blame elsewhere – 'it's because he was neutered' or 'we hardly feed her anything, it must be the way she is' – but, in fact, obesity in dogs is always the fault of the owner and never the dog. That might sound harsh but, if this problem is going to be tackled effectively, it is imperative that dog owners realise their responsibility is to keep their dogs in shape, and that, if their dogs are overweight, the blame lies with them rather than their dogs. We, the owners, are in total control of the amount of food our dog eats and the amount of energy he expends in exercise, so a problem such as obesity, which is driven almost exclusively by these two factors, is clearly a problem that can be prevented and controlled by the owner.

Of course, this is somewhat of an oversimplification of matters and if it was that straightforward there wouldn't be an obesity problem, and there clearly is one. Dog owners are people and people don't always work in a logical manner, with an infinite number of psychological influences affecting decision making. At the most extreme end of the spectrum, this can lead to a form of body dysmorphia projected on to dogs, making the owner see their dog as underweight when in fact they are grossly overweight. In most cases, it is more subtle, such as anthropomorphism where the owner identifies too closely with the dog's feelings, particularly hunger, or misplaced affection confusing feeding with love or attention. These 'owner factors' are one of the main reasons why we see so many overweight pets. The other main reason is lack of awareness about obesity and its related health problems and this can be a contributing factor in many cases.

I never cease to be amazed by the number of owners who profess to be surprised when I tell them that their dog is overweight or even obese. Some may be feigning surprise to mitigate responsibility for the problem, but there is definitely a significant proportion of people to whom the diagnosis is a genuine surprise, despite their dog often being clearly overweight. Part of this goes back to what I describe as the body-dysmorphia issue where people simply don't see their pets as overweight, but much of this problem comes down to lack of education about obesity in dogs. We can usually tell from a simple glance if a person is overweight or not, but the same is by no means true when it comes to assessing the weight of our pets. This probably comes down to the fact that we are simply not accustomed to making this kind of judgement about a completely different species, with their different body shape and a thick covering of hair disguising much of the body outline.

So can you tell if your dog is overweight or not? Well, there are various methods, including the obvious route of simply weighing your dog, but the most accurate and reliable technique is what's known as condition scoring. This process has the advantage of offering a qualitative assessment of the dog's body, independent from their breed, size and actual weight. The problem with relying on a purely quantitative method such as weighing is that it requires interpretation based on an ideal weight – and who really can say with any degree of accuracy what the ideal weight is for their dog? As a vet I give estimates for people of the ideal weight of their dog, but these are rough guesses based on my personal views and experience rather than anything more scientific. Another vet might agree that the dog is overweight but give a very different value for their ideal target weight, making assessing the degree of obesity based on weight alone prone to error.

Condition scoring involves assessing the dog's body based on criteria including fat coverage, shape and prominence of underlying skeletal features, to give a score based on a scale, usually 1–5 (although some condition-scoring scales are more detailed and include up to ten different scores). My personal favourite approach is a simple scale from 1 to 5 based on assessing the following key features – fat coverage over the ribs, presence or absence of a waist behind the ribs if viewed from above, prominence or not of the hip bones and size of the abdomen. If you consider your dog's body based on these criteria, you should be able to decide which of the following classifications best describes the condition of your dog:

1. Emaciated

   It is easy to see your dog's ribs, lumbar vertebrae, pelvic bones and all body prominences from a distance. There is no obvious body fat and clear evidence of muscle wastage.

2. Thin

   While you cannot easily see the ribs and the pelvic bones are not obviously prominent from a distance, your dog's ribs are easily felt with no palpable fat. The tops of lumbar vertebrae are visible and there is an obvious abdominal tuck behind the ribs, as well as a clear waist when viewed from above.

3. Normal

   A normal dog should have a distinct but not excessive covering of fat over the chest, through which the ribs are easily palpable. The abdomen is tucked up when viewed from the side, and there is a visible but not extensive waist when viewed from above. The pelvis and other bony prominences are well covered and not clearly visible.

4. Overweight

   A dog that is overweight will generally be carrying up to 20 per cent extra weight compared to their normal state which is generally laid down around the chest and abdomen, making it hard to feel the ribs, and giving the abdomen a full appearance, with little or no abdominal tuck. There is also very little or no waist visible from above, and there may also be obvious fatty deposits in the lumbar region and around the base of the tail.

5. Obese

Dogs carrying more than 20 per cent extra weight are classified as obese. These dogs will have large fat deposits over their chest, neck, spine and tail base. They have no waist or abdominal tuck behind the ribs, and their abdomens often appear distended. As well as appearing clearly overweight, their movement will also be affected by their weight, giving them a shortened stride and splayed leg appearance as their legs are forced outwards by fatty deposits.

Undertaking the process of condition scoring is usually very illuminating and makes it easy for a dog owner to appreciate the fact that their dog really is overweight by demonstrating physically the excess fat on the body. This tends to be a much more effective approach than simply saying 'your dog is 5kg overweight' as it makes the owner really take a close look at their dog, which is something that too many owners fail to do (or rather they look but don't see, as the old saying goes).

Having established that a dog is overweight or obese, the next big step is doing something about it. This usually involves some kind of diet and exercise plan, often put together under the supervision of a vet or veterinary nurse. It is well worth involving your vets in any weight-loss programme you decide to implement, especially if your dog is severely overweight, as losing weight can be a hazardous process with some health risks to be considered. The main considerations are the rate of weight loss and the ultimate target weight. The rate of weight loss is an issue because, if you put your dog on a crash diet where they lose lots of weight very quickly, this can lead to health complications such as fatty deposits in the liver (although this is more common in cats), so it is advisable to stick to a moderate rate of 1–1.5 per cent per week as a safe maximum. So this would equate to a weight loss of between 300 and 450g per week for a 30kg dog, meaning that it would take around three months for this dog to safely lose 5kg.

The issue of ultimate target weight is more subjective, as previously discussed, and should always be kept in context with the concurrent use of condition scoring as a fail-safe back-up. For example, if your vet advises that your 30kg dog needs to lose 5kg to get to a target weight of 25kg, it might be that at 26kg a condition-score exercise determines that your dog is actually now at a 'normal' weight and the weight-loss programme can be stopped rather than continuing to the arbitrary figure of 25kg. Always be prepared to modify your target based on the physical evidence of condition scoring as this is a much more reliable and safe guide to your dog's true state of weight than simply relying on what the scales say.

There are many approaches to effecting weight loss in dogs, ranging from simply feeding less and walking more to the use of expensive 'prescription' diets, ie diets formulated specifically to aid weight loss in obese dogs, but, whatever approach you choose, there are some key pieces of advice to consider:

DIET

Eating too much of the wrong kind of food is the main reason that so many pets are overweight. By making some simple changes to the way you feed your pet, you can make a big difference to their weight and wellbeing:

- Reduce the calories – The ideal way to keep your pet slim is to feed them exactly the right amount of calories (or energy) every day. If they are overweight, then you simply need to feed less, or use a lower-calorie food, and they will lose weight. Your vet will be able to give you detailed guidance, but generally reducing their total daily calories by around 20 per cent is ideal.

Joe's Recipe Book

LOW-FAT TREATS

Most dogs live for their treats and tit-bits, so cutting them out completely can be a huge challenge when trying to put an overweight dog on a diet. This low-fat recipe is a great way of being able to still give your dog the occasional snack or treat without adding too many calories to his daily intake.

To make a batch of biscuits, you will need:
250ml (1/2 pt) hot water
1 beef stock cube
2 tablespoons olive oil
500g wholewheat flour
1 stick celery, finely chopped
1 carrot, grated (no need to peel)

Dissolve the stock cube in the hot water and add to the flour and vegetables in a large mixing bowl. Add the stock gradually to form a thick dough, which you can roll out on a well-floured surface until it is about 1cm thick. Then cut out small biscuit shapes using a knife or the end of an apple corer. Try to make the biscuits a little bit smaller than normal – every little helps when it comes to cutting down the calories!

Place the biscuits on a greased baking tray and cook in a moderate oven for about half an hour. Allow to cool and ration with steely determination! (Store in the fridge in an airtight container for several weeks.)

- Cut out the tit-bits – Leftovers and tit-bits from the table are the number-one enemy of slim pets! We tend to give the least healthy bits from our meals, such as fatty bits of meat, and these go straight from your plate on to your pet's hips!
- Use healthy fillers – Grated vegetables such as carrots or courgettes add bulk to food but very few calories so they are a good way of keeping your pet feeling full but not piling on the pounds.
- Small regular meals – Better than one big meal, so divide your dog's food into two small meals, morning and evening.
- Choose a healthy food – Avoid 'junk foods' containing high levels of sugars, fats and artificial additives.

EXERCISE

Along with a suitable diet, regular and appropriate exercise is vital to keep your dog in shape.

- Build up gradually – Don't suddenly change the amount of exercise your dog gets as this could cause health problems. Instead, make the change gradually over a few weeks to let them adjust to the new regime, especially if they are old or very overweight.

- Make it fun – Exercise regimes are so much easier to stick to if they are fun, so choose something that you and your pet will enjoy. Why not consider joining your local flyball club, or try mountain biking or jogging with your dog, as activities like this can be a great way of burning off calories as well as being fun for all concerned.

- Take it easy – If your pet is old or suffers from a mobility problem such as arthritis, it's important not to overdo it. Regular short walks are much better for older dogs than long hikes, and make sure you talk to your vet if you are concerned about any lameness or stiffness associated with increased exercise.

GENERAL WEIGHT-LOSS TIPS

- Don't give in to begging – Dogs who beg will never be satisfied so, even if you do give them the treat they want, they will still want more. Much better to be firm and only give them healthy snacks at set times such as just before bedtime.

- Give your pet attention, not treats – Many owners use

food as a reward and a way of 'buying' affection from their pets – use attention as a reward instead by spending quality time with your pet.

- Portion control – You are not being cruel by cutting down their food! A healthy, slim dog will be much happier than an overweight one.
- Dry food is much more filling than it looks – Dry dog food swells up when it reaches the stomach, so what looks like a tiny portion will still fill your pet up.
- Neutering does not cause obesity! – Many people worry that their pet will become overweight if they are neutered, and, while it is true that neutering can slow the metabolism and reduce the amount of calories a pet needs, that doesn't mean that this should automatically lead to weight gain, as you can easily reduce the amount of calories they eat and ensure that they have an active lifestyle to compensate for this.

Joe's TV Casebook

FAT PETS ON *THIS MORNING*
Over the years I've been a 'TV vet' I've discussed the issue of obesity on more programmes than I care to remember, from *Blue Peter* to *The One Show*, but the most memorable time was on *This Morning* on ITV. The item featured three overweight pets, who were all taking part in the PDSA 'Pet Fit Club' challenge where the charity helps some of the most overweight pets to lose weight through a concentrated and

closely monitored weight-loss programme. The pets that joined me on the *This Morning* sofa included a Labrador who tipped the scales some 15kg above his ideal weight, a rotund Jack Russell who'd entirely lost his zest for life since he'd put on over 4kg after being neutered, and a cat that was nearly double his ideal weight of 4kg.

The reason this was such a memorable item for me was not that the pets all disgraced themselves on live TV, or that their owners were particularly entertaining, but it was simply because, between the three pets in the studio, I was able to demonstrate almost the entire range of reasons for pets becoming obese. Firstly there was Harvey the Labrador whose problem was that he simply ate too much and was over-indulged by his owner who was trying to compensate for his bad start in life (he was abused by his previous owner) by giving him love in the form of leftovers and extra treats. Then there was the Jack Russell, who put on weight after being neutered and entered a vicious cycle of weight gain, less exercise and more weight gain. And finally the enormously overweight cat whose problem was not excessive consumption but inadequate exercise – he simply never budged from the sofa!

With these three different but very typical cases, I was able to demonstrate to the viewers the basic problems that lead to obesity in pets – overeating, failure to compensate for lifestyle changes and under-exercising. And, as well as being a great opportunity to get some key messages across to millions of pet owners, it was also great fun, particularly when the presenter, Eamonn Holmes, attempted to get the lazy cat to show interest in a fishing-rod cat toy and the cat gave him one of those disdainful looks that only cats can carry off!

ARTHRITIS

Many dogs suffer from arthritis in one form or another. It is a major source of pain, discomfort and mobility problems for hundreds of thousands of dogs in the UK alone. The term 'arthritis' simply means 'inflammation of a joint' and therefore it can be used to refer to a wide range of conditions, including septic arthritis, which is a bacterial joint infection, rheumatoid arthritis, an autoimmune form of joint disease where a malfunction of the immune system leads to damage of the cartilage lining the joints, and traumatic arthritis, where physical injuries to a joint lead to inflammation and joint disease. However, for the purposes of this discussion, I am going to use the term to refer to the most common form of joint disease seen in dogs – osteoarthritis, or OA.

Osteoarthritis is a wide-ranging condition in its own right, with many contributing factors, but in general terms refers to joint disease caused by mechanical issues such as those caused by poor physical conformation, or problems in the growth and development of a joint. An unstable or badly formed joint inevitably wears more quickly than a perfectly formed joint, and this wear and tear leads directly to damage to the cartilage lining the joint, and indirectly to one of the major secondary problems associated with arthritis which is new bone formation. The production of new bony spurs and fragments around an unstable or badly formed joint occurs because of the body's inappropriate reaction to the primary instability or malformation, and can be one of the main causes of the pain and restriction of mobility seen in these cases. In the most advanced cases, new bone formation can render a joint practically unusable through a combination of pain and simple physical restriction to movement, leading to very severe consequences for the dog – even, in the most extreme instances, euthanasia on compassionate grounds, although this is much less common nowadays thanks to advances in treatment.

Arthritis can affect dogs of all ages, from adolescence to old age, and, although some breeds are more prone than others, a dog of any size can be affected. It has many clinical manifestations, but those most commonly encountered in domestic dogs are:

- Hip dysplasia – Probably the best-known and most prevalent arthritic condition seen in dogs, involving a deformity of the hip joint. In a normal hip, the ball at the end of the femur (thigh bone) fits snugly deep into the hip socket in the pelvis. In cases of hip dysplasia, however, the joint is badly formed with the ball often just resting on the edge of a shallow or almost non-existent socket, and this leads to instability, pain and restricted movement, all of which are compounded as new bone is formed around the joint.

- Shoulder and elbow dysplasia – Although not as common as hip dysplasia, deformities in other joints, particularly the shoulder and elbow, do occur and can lead to equally serious consequences.

- OCD – Osteochondrosis dessicans is a clinical condition usually affecting the elbow joint, and involves problems with the development and maintenance of the cartilage in the joint, which often leads to subsequent osteoarthritis and all the associated problems of pain and restricted movement.

• Arthritis secondary to injury – After the developmental causes of arthritis such as hip dysplasia and OCD, the next most common cause of joint disease is injury, and the most common example of this arthritis is as a consequence of ligament rupture in the knee (or stifle joint, as it is known in animals).

Rupture of the cranial cruciate ligament is a very common injury in dogs, as well as being the classic footballer's injury among humans (probably the most famous case was the injury that led to the end of Paul Gascoigne's career as a footballer). The cruciate ligaments hold the knee together, preventing the femur (thigh bone) and tibia (shin bone) from moving backwards and forwards in relation to each other. When the knee is subject to severe abnormal forces, these ligaments can snap, making the joint instantly unstable – and very painful. This instability does not lead to instant osteoarthritis, but, even after the ligament has been repaired (which is usually the course of action recommended in dogs), it is inevitable that the joint will develop arthritic changes over the coming years. In most cases, these changes can be minimised by prompt and appropriate treatment at an early stage, but, in a significant proportion, the original injury leads to a lifetime of mild to moderate arthritic pain and movement restriction.

There are many contributing causes to these types of arthritis, and, as with everything in this book, I try to take a holistic approach and consider all factors, including those related to the lifestyle of the dog and relationship with their owner, which are, in my view, often overlooked. The big factors that contribute to arthritis in dogs are, in order of significance, genetics, lifestyle and luck – and I will now take a look at each of these in more detail.

GENETICS

The genetic make-up and phenotypic (ie physical) expression of these genes are the most significant factors in many developmental disorders that lead to arthritis, such as hip dysplasia and OCD. These conditions occur because of physical problems in the development or 'design' of the joints, and it is the genes and their expression in the body that control these factors. Lifestyle issues do have a significant role to play in many of these conditions, but the most important factor is nearly always the physical make-up of the joint and the way in which it develops as the puppy matures into an adult dog.

It is worth mentioning at this point that the vast majority of these conditions are not seen in wild dogs and are by-products of the domestication process. Evolution is a harsh task master and any genetic variations that increased the risk of crippling disorders such as hip dysplasia would quickly be selected against and eliminated from the gene pool. It is only since we humans came into the picture and started selecting

271

artificially for traits such as domesticity and physical appearance, and removed the pressure of natural selection, that such conditions were able to establish themselves in the canine population. The effect of removing natural selection pressure is amplified by our desire to create dogs with very specific physical features, such as German Shepherds with low hips, or Dachshunds with very long backs. Unintentional it may be, but the consequence of selecting for many of these physical traits has been the subsequent development of physical deformities such as dysplastic hip. Until this fact is appreciated by the breeders and show judges who determine the direction that breed standards take, we will never win the battle against these eminently preventable yet crippling disorders.

LIFESTYLE

As previously discussed in the chapter about adolescence, the way we raise our dogs can play a major role in the long-term health of their joints, particularly developmental conditions such as OCD. Excessive growth rates and over-exercise at a young age can both put extra stresses and strains on the joints, and dramatically increase the likelihood of arthritic changes developing in those joints. Therefore, it is vital that you are aware of these issues and take steps to prevent any complications linked to these lifestyle factors early on as damage done at this time will generally be irreparable and lead to a lifetime of pain and discomfort.

Adolescence is one of the times when lifestyle factors

play a big role in arthritic conditions, but it is by no means the only time of life when you need to be aware of how your daily routines with your dog can impact on his joints. Old age is another time of life when over-exercise can contribute to ongoing joint damage and therefore pain, but, even in the prime of your dog's life, it is important to remember how his everyday exercise can impact the health of his joints. A dog with mild underlying hip dysplasia or a slightly arthritic elbow may be fine if restricted to short walks, but deteriorate significantly if taken on ten-mile hikes or enrolled in a flyball class for example. It's all about knowing your dog and understanding his limitations – and creating a lifestyle with him that suits his need to exercise without putting undue strain on his joints. There's nothing worse than incapacitating a dog through over-exercise simply because you can't say no to his demands for walks. Always think long term and remember that a slightly put-out dog now because he only got 15 minutes in the field rather than 30 will live a longer and happier life than the same dog who over-did it and spends the rest of his days with sore legs.

As well as exercise, the other obvious lifestyle factor to consider is weight and feeding. Every extra pound your dog carries will put an extra load on his joints and be likely to cause more pain and more ongoing damage, so it's really important that any dog with joint problems is carefully maintained at their optimum weight.

Lifestyle factors are important to consider with any dog that has a history of joint problems, no matter how minor, and your vet is the best person to advise both on exercise regimes and weight control. In general, though, there are a couple of key points to remember, particularly in regard to exercising a dog with arthritis:

- Early diagnosis is vital, so look out for the first signs of arthritis, which include stiffness after exercise, reluctance to jump or climb stairs, lameness on one or more legs and general lethargy and depression.
- Several short walks a day are better than one or two long walks.
- Avoid activities that put extra stress and strain on the joints such as chasing sticks or balls.
- Make sure your dog has a warm and dry bed as the cold and damp exacerbate arthritic pain in dogs just as with people.
- Keep a very close eye on your dog's weight.

Joe's Surgery Casebook

WILSON'S LEG

'Oh my poor little boy,' cried Wilson's owner, a larger-than-life character called Jane, who I knew from previous experience was totally devoted to her little crossbreed Terrier (he'd once been brought in because Jane was worried that he was looking a little depressed and insisted that he have blood tests and a vitamin injection even though there was nothing clinically wrong with him!). 'He ran off after a rabbit and came back holding his leg up.'

As soon as I saw Wilson hopping around on three legs, I suspected a classic injury that is caused by this kind of incident – a ruptured cruciate ligament – and, sure enough, a quick examination of his knee confirmed that this was indeed the case.

'I'm sorry to say Wilson's going to need an operation,' I explained, steeling myself for the inevitable histrionics that I knew would follow – and I wasn't disappointed!

'Oh my God, an operation? Are you sure he needs it? What about the anaesthetic? Will he be OK? Oh my poor little darling!' gushed Jane, embracing her dog emotionally.

It took a while but I eventually managed to calm her down and booked Wilson in for his operation first thing the following week when I knew I'd be back in the surgery. In the meantime, I bandaged his leg and gave Jane a course of painkillers to give him over the weekend.

Before I was back in the surgery to do the operation, I was off to London for my regular spot on *The Wright Stuff* on Five. The show went well, with a couple of interesting questions from viewers including one about a prima donna parrot who was refusing food, and, coincidentally, a dog with a bag leg. Then it was back to the surgery to prepare for Wilson's operation the following day.

Cruciate operations are always quite stressful (well, for me, anyway) and this one was trickier than normal, with a couple of technical problems to overcome before I was happy with the end result. Thankfully, Wilson came round absolutely fine and was bouncing in his kennel by the time a very relieved Jane came to pick him up in the evening. I think he should go on to make a full recovery provided he gets plenty of rest – something that might be easier said than done knowing Wilson's character!

LUCK

Like it or not, but lady luck plays a big role in all of our lives, and our dogs are no different. In the case of arthritis, the main way luck plays a role is through accidents and incidents which damage joints and lead to arthritis. The classic example of this is the cruciate ligament injury, which, although influenced by genetic factors (some breeds are much more prone to this problem than others), is also largely a factor of luck, as, like most physical injuries, it's down to a mixture of circumstances coming together.

DIAGNOSIS AND TREATMENT

After considering how and why arthritis occurs, the next subject to cover is the diagnosis of arthritic conditions, which is not always as straightforward as you may think. The typical clinical symptoms of arthritis are lameness and reluctance to use the affected limbs. These symptoms are also seen with a wide range of other conditions including muscle or ligament strains, bruises and traumatic injuries such as cuts to the pads. A thorough clinical examination by a vet should eliminate the obvious possibilities such as wounds, but distinguishing between arthritis and a soft-tissue injury such as a sprain or bruise can be very hard by examination alone. In most cases, the vet will use more than his clinical examination to help make a diagnosis, considering the dog's age, breed and medical history as well as information from the owner regarding the duration, rapidness of onset and timing of the symptoms – but even so, unless there are really clear physical symptoms such as crepitus (the grinding feeling of a joint with poor conformation and new bone formation) or joint swelling, it is usually impossible to make a diagnosis of arthritis with any degree of certainty unless additional tests are undertaken.

The most widely used procedure to make a firm diagnosis of arthritis is the x-ray. Radiology has been used for many decades to take pictures of bones and is still the number-one technique of choice for routine imaging of bones and joints in people as well as animals. A good x-ray will clearly show arthritic changes in a joint such as new bone formation, as well as often offering evidence for underlying causes such as joint deformities, and it is usually the only diagnostic procedure required in most cases.

In more complex situations, particularly in referral clinics where dogs are being assessed for complex surgical procedures, or subtle joint changes are being assessed to make a difficult diagnosis, more advanced techniques are used. The main one available for dogs is the computed tomography (CT) scan. This is really just a very advanced x-ray machine that provides a three-dimensional view of bony structures including joints. CT scans are expensive and only available in a limited number of clinics, but they offer unparalleled diagnostic information that can be critical in difficult cases.

With a diagnosis of arthritis made, the next step to consider is how we treat this condition. As you might expect with such a complex and wide-ranging condition, there are numerous treatment options to consider for arthritic dogs, ranging from the very simplest – rest – to the most complex – joint-replacement surgery. The principal treatment options for arthritic dogs are:

REST AND RECUPERATION

A little 'R&R' is often the best treatment for mild cases of arthritis. It's amazing how well the body can deal with most medical conditions if only given the time to do so, and, in the case of arthritic joints, the longer they are rested and not stressed or strained, the better. With a well-maintained programme of rest and recuperation, many arthritis cases will settle down so ongoing pain and discomfort can be effectively managed in the long term.

PAINKILLERS AND ANTI-INFLAMMATORY DRUGS

In the majority of cases that end up at the vets, routine painkilling and anti-inflammatory drugs are prescribed alongside a programme of rest and recuperation. The most commonly used drugs are known as non-steroidal anti-inflammatories or NSAIDS and these include the drugs Carprofen and Meloxicam. They are generally safe (although there are some safety issues to bear in mind, particularly in older animals) and can be very effective in controlling mild to moderate pain.

Other drugs that can also be used include steroids, which have generally been superseded by NSAIDS due to their side-effects, and some opiate painkillers which are used in conjunction with NSAIDS in more serious cases. There is also a popular injection called Cartrophen which acts to promote cartilage repair that is commonly used by vets, usually as an initial course of four weekly injections followed by occasional top-up injections. It is a little hit-and-miss, doing nothing in some cases but occasionally proving very effective, so worth a try but by no means guaranteed to succeed.

SUPPLEMENTS AND COMPLEMENTARY THERAPIES

Since their introduction to human medicine in the early nineties, joint supplements such as glucosamine and chondroitin have become widely accepted and used in treating arthritis in dogs as well. Glucosamine and chondroitin are natural molecules that aid the repair and maintenance of joint cartilage which have been shown to have clearly beneficial effects on dogs with clinical arthritis problems, so I personally recommend that all arthritic dogs should be taking these supplements, finances permitting.

In addition to glucosamine and chondroitin, there are various other natural supplements and remedies that have varying degrees of efficacy – and even more widely varying amounts of proof behind the claims made by their manufacturers. Turmeric powder has been shown to have anti-inflammatory properties and is incorporated in several leading joint supplements for dogs, but many other approaches such as homeopathic remedies, magnetic collars and copper bracelets are all lacking in scientific evidence and should be treated with caution – particularly as many of these so-called therapies are not cheap!

SURGERY

The ultimate treatment option for arthritis is the surgeon's knife. This is usually the last resort in cases that have not responded to medical therapy, and should always be viewed with caution as, whatever the surgeons may tell you, there is always a risk with any surgical procedure and no guarantees. It's important that you fully understand the risks as well as potential benefits of any operation before signing your dog up for surgery.

There are many different operations used to treat arthritic conditions, but they all aim to either improve the conformation or stability of an existing joint, or replace an arthritic joint with a new, artificial one. The most common operations available are:

- Arthroscopy – A relatively simple procedure that involves making a small incision over the affected joint and carrying out procedures such as removing debris using a camera and forceps. Arthroscopy is also often used as a diagnostic procedure to provide visual evidence for damage to structure such as cartilage that do not appear clearly on x-rays. The risks associated with this kind of procedure are generally low – but not entirely absent as joint infections are not unknown after arthroscopy operations – yet the scope of repairs is also limited with only specific, and generally relatively minor, problems being appropriate for this approach.
- Cruciate ligament repairs – Rupture of the cranial cruciate ligament is a common problem. Effective treatment is vital if the initial injury isn't to lead to

significant long-term joint disease. There are a wide range of operations available for this purpose, and I could fill an entire book if I were to go into full detail on each, but the general principles are relatively simple to explain.

The most basic form of repair is called an external stabilisation, a procedure that attempts to replace the ligament outside the joint using a thick nylon or wire suture placed between the front of the tibia and back of the femur. Despite being the simplest of the surgical options, it is reasonably effective, particularly in smaller dogs, and is often the treatment of choice in first opinion veterinary practices.

Next in the scale of complexity is a rather old-fashioned operation called an 'over the top' repair, involving replacement of the ligament inside the joint using a strip of tissue cut from the outside of the thigh muscle. When I first qualified as a vet back in the mid-90s, this was the most common operation used to repair cruciate ligament injuries, and can have a very good success rate if done well. However, it has largely been superseded by the simpler and usually equally effective external stabilisation operation and, increasingly, by the more complex operations that are now relatively commonplace.

The most important of these more complex operations is the tibial plateaux levelling operation (TPLO), a technically demanding operation carried out exclusively by orthopaedic specialists. The science behind it is based on complex bio-mechanics, but essentially it aims to tilt the top of the tibia to counteract the forces against which the cranial cruciate ligament usually works.

If your dog does have the misfortune to rupture his cruciate ligament, it can be daunting trying to choose between these treatment options – listen to your own vet and they might recommend an external stabilisation (or an over the top if they're of a certain age!), but talk to a referral specialist and they will almost certainly strongly recommend TPLO. The key thing to remember is that, despite claims and counterclaims, there is actually very little evidence to say which of these procedures gives the best result. At best, there is some evidence that a TPLO reduces the recovery time, but the ultimate outcome is very similar whichever operation you choose. The priority is to work with a vet you trust and let them guide you to the most suitable option for you and your dog.

• Triple Pelvic Osteotomy (TPO) – This is a well-established procedure aimed at improving the stability of dysplastic hip joints in adolescent dogs. It involves making three cuts in the bones of the pelvis and rotating the free segment so that the socket of the hip joint is better aligned with the ball of the femur. It is a major operation and carries with it the possibility of a range of serious complications, but it is also a relatively routine operation that is carried out regularly by experienced orthopaedic surgeons which minimises the risks involved.

- Hip replacement – Although this may sound a bit over the top for dogs, the advent of joint-replacement operations in veterinary surgery has provided a realistic treatment option in the most severe cases of joint disease and given a new lease of life to thousands of dogs. The hip joint is the most common candidate for replacement, and this is now a relatively routine operation offered in severe cases of hip dysplasia. Just as with human beings, the operation involves removing the entire hip joint and replacing it with an artificial one, usually made from titanium. The operation is technically demanding and only carried out by orthopaedic specialists in referral centres. It carries with it all the risks you might expect from such a major operation – implant failure, infection, bone fractures and so on. Having said that, the benefits certainly outweigh the risks in the more serious cases where no other treatment options exist.

- Excision arthroplasty – This operation involves simply removing the affected joint. It is the procedure of last resort. Although the term could refer to the surgical removal of any joint, in practice this term is used for the operation to remove the ball of the hip joint. This operation, which sounds counter-intuitive and unlikely to help, is actually usually remarkably successful and I have seen many dogs regain near-perfect pain-free mobility after an excision arthroplasty operation. The logic of the procedure is that having no joint is better than having a painful joint, and, by removing the source of pain and mobility restriction, the operation immediately improves the quality of life for the patient. The big issue that owners tend to struggle with is understanding how a dog can still walk on a leg with no hip joint. They're not the only ones who find this operation surprising: to this day, after carrying out this procedure many times, I'm still amazed at the way in which the body copes with such a massive trauma and effectively forms a new joint from fibrous scar tissue. It is undertaken mainly in smaller dogs and cats where the mechanical forces are not quite so significant, and when a fibrous joint is sufficiently strong to support the weight of the dog, but it is still one of the more remarkable procedures we carry out – and one that can make a very big difference to the quality of life of the patient.

There may be many treatment options available for arthritic dogs, but unfortunately effective treatment is not always possible, and the long-term effects of joint disease can be very debilitating and lead to significant quality of life issues. Dogs live to exercise, and therefore it's not just the physical pain that's an issue, it's also the psychological effect of not being able to live life to the full. My theory is that dogs have a kind of work ethic that drives them to get out and run, so being unable to fulfil this naturally driven behaviour must inevitably lead to frustration and unhappiness.

Therefore, before we leave this subject, it's worth underlining the absolute importance of prevention when it comes to arthritis – and the key things to remember in this respect are:

- Choose your dog well – Always ask breeders for hip score certificates which show that the sire and dame of your dog have better hips than the breed averages (a lower number is better – aim for single figures if possible). This is not an absolute guarantee, but does give you a much better chance of avoiding dogs with severe hip dysplasia. If you're not set on one particular breed, do some research and choose a breed without known joint problems, or, better still, go for a crossbreed as they are generally much less likely to suffer from genetically inherited joint problems.
- Bring your dog up well – Think carefully about the amount of exercise your dog gets during their adolescence, and make sure they are on a suitable diet.

EIGHT

The End of the Relationship – Old Age

Old age comes to us all, and our dogs are obviously no exception. Unlike humans, who tend to age gradually over many years – if not decades – the effects of ageing generally are felt more suddenly in dogs. Many dogs look and behave in exactly the same way until they reach a certain age, perhaps ten or eleven years, when suddenly their bodies seem to realise that they are in fact getting old. All the changes one would expect – grey hair, stiff joints, failing eyesight and so on – come along at once and the dog almost becomes old overnight.

Of course, it's not usually quite that dramatic, but I guess, because of the relatively short life spans of dogs when compared to people, it's no surprise that we should find their ageing process to be more rapid than our own. There's probably also an element of owners not wanting to see that their best friend is getting old, and a little denial playing a role until the changes are too obvious to ignore.

Before getting on to some of the issues that face our dogs as they get older, it's worth just taking the time to consider what old really is for a dog, and how much it can vary between dogs of different breeds. For example, a small breed such as a Terrier might well get into his teens before we'd consider him old, whereas a giant dog such as a Great Dane could be considered old by the time he is six or seven.

To get an idea of how old a dog is, many people like to think in human terms, and the classic approach is to work on the premise that a single dog year equates to seven human years – so a five-year-old dog is roughly 35 in human terms. This is all very well for an average-sized dog, but it doesn't work at all for dogs at either end of the size spectrum, as their life expectancies are so different. To get round this issue, I've devised a slightly more complicated system that gives a more accurate picture of how old dogs of all shapes and sizes are in human terms:

- For little dogs (up to 10kg) – 12 human years per dog year for the first two years, and then 4 per year thereafter. So a 10-year-old terrier will be 56 and a 15-year-old will be 76.
- For medium dogs (10–30kg) – 10 human years per dog year for the first two years, and then 5 per year thereafter. A 10-year-old spaniel, for example, will be 60 and a 15-year-old will be 85.
- For big dogs (30kg +) – A bit simpler, 8 human years per dog year all the way. So an 8-year-old German Shepherd will be roughly 64 in human terms.

Age has many effects on the canine body, but it's not just the physical side of things that change as dogs get older, for their minds will also change. The mental and physical effects of age will impact on the relationship between owner and dog. Older dogs will tend to be slower, both physically and mentally, and this will affect their everyday routines and may also change the way in which you interact with your dog. When your dog was young and fit, your life with him would have been full of energetic activities enjoyed together, but now he's struggling to get about, the time you spend together is more likely to be on the sofa rather than in the park. This is necessarily a problem, but something to be aware of as your dog ages. You need to appreciate that an older dog isn't the pup he once was, and, although he may still try his best to keep up and chase the sticks you throw for him, inside he will be creaking and groaning and dreaming of a nap by the fireside!

Adjusting your lifestyle to suit the changing needs of your dog as he gets older is the best way in which you can maintain a healthy relationship with your dog. It's well worth having a thorough check-up at your vets at least once a year, as this will enable your vet to give you early warning of any old-age health problems that might be developing. This is not only useful in terms of prevention and treatment, it's also important in helping you appreciate the fact that your dog really is getting older and perhaps it's time to make some changes to help him get the best out of life as he ages.

Making changes to your lifestyle to help your older dog cope is simply about thinking through his daily routine and identifying any areas of his life that might be being affected by his age, then considering how you could make changes that might improve his quality of life. Here are some of my suggestions for simple ways to improve the life of an older dog:

Sleeping arrangements – Older dogs are often prone to aches and pains, especially when the weather is cold and wet, so it's important to consider where they sleep and whether or not the location and actual bed itself is suitable. Make sure their bed is in a warm, draft-free part of the house – or, if they live out, that their kennel is weather-proof and suitably sheltered from the wind – and consider replacing their bed if it's old and worn, as a new bed can make a big difference to an older dog. As well as considering a standard bed, it can be worth thinking about a more luxurious option such as a memory-foam bed or specialist orthopaedic bed if your dog suffers from joint problems.

Exercise regime – How and where you exercise your dog as he gets older is one of the more important factors when it comes to his quality of life – too much strenuous exercise and he'll struggle to keep up and be at risk of exacerbating joint problems; too little and he'll become frustrated and potentially overweight. Getting the balance right is not always easy, but in general the best approach is, as always, to listen to what your dog is telling you. Read his body language and observe him after exercise to see how it's affected him, and use that information to help you gauge how much exercise suits him at his particular time of life.

It's also an area your vet can help you with, particularly if your dog is suffering from a medical condition that is likely to impact on his exercise regime, such as arthritis or heart disease.

Diet – Diet is another factor that can play a big role in the health and happiness of an older dog. As dogs age, their requirements for some of the basic nutrients such as protein change and it is generally best to consider changing to a diet aimed at senior dogs once they reach around 50 in human years. Senior diets are usually lower in protein and also have restricted levels of phosphorus and salt, as well as added ingredients such as glucosamine and chondroitin to help with joint problems.

In addition to the make-up of the food itself, it's also worth thinking about how, when and where you feed it. Older dogs often lose their sense of smell as they age which can affect their appetite as palatability is largely driven by smell. To counter this, you can try warming wet foods slightly to release more of their smell, or add a tasty gravy to a dry food. Where and when you feed can also be important as older dogs often benefit from eating off a raised step or platform to aid their digestion, and may also be happier eating more small meals rather than fewer larger ones – some owners feed their dogs three or four times a day when they are older as this seems to help them maintain their overall appetite and improve their digestion.

Keep their brains active – Just because your dog is getting on doesn't mean they can't still enjoy, and benefit from, mental stimulation. The old saying 'you can't teach an old dog new tricks' is all very well, but it doesn't mean there's no benefit in trying! Dogs of all ages love attention and stimulation, and giving an older dog a new challenge such as a session of advanced training classes or learning a new trick can be a really effective way of improving their quality of life.

No matter how well you look after an older dog, there always comes the time when age catches up with them and the end of their days draws near. This last topic of discussion is a sensitive one and, as well as being a difficult subject for dog owners to consider, it also represents one of the most challenging aspects of the job of a small-animal vet. Vets have to face the incredibly difficult process of advising dog owners during those final months, weeks and days, and ultimately helping to make the final decision to bring a treasured pet's life to an end.

One of the most common questions people ask when they discover I'm a vet is 'How do you cope when you have to put animals to sleep?' I usually respond that, in fact, while it can be a very stressful and upsetting part of the job, in many ways I see it as one of the most valuable services vets provide. It might sound strange for a professional who is dedicated to saving animals to view ending their lives as a valuable service, but, as with so many aspects of our lives with our dogs, things tend to make more sense if we think about them from the dog's perspective.

In the case of euthanasia, the reason why I feel it can be positive and a valuable part of the services provided by vets is that it is really the most effective way of ending suffering and pain. Drugs and surgery are all very well and can help minimise the symptoms of serious illness and improve the quality of and prolong life, but in many cases our patients reach a point where it is clear that they are beyond the help of the medical and surgical treatments we have available and that there is no hope of recovery. At this stage, when an animal is clearly suffering, whether physically or mentally (or both), and there is no realistic hope of recovery, we have to think about the wellbeing of the dog and see the situation from their perspective. Dogs, like many animals, seem to know when they are dying. When this point is reached, euthanasia offers a wonderfully swift and pain-free alternative to letting nature take its often prolonged and therefore unpleasant course.

The process of euthanasia is nearly always harder on the owner than the patient. Again, this might sound like a strange statement given that the patient is going to die, but, again, thinking about it from the dog's perspective offers a very different viewpoint. Dogs don't have a great capacity for anticipation – they tend to live in the here and now and worry about the future when it arrives. This lack of ability to think about what is to come is a great asset when considering euthanasia. Instead of being aware of what is going to happen for days or even weeks beforehand as the owners are, the dog is thinking no more than a few hours ahead each day. So, when it comes to that final injection in the vet's consulting room or at home, the dog has no idea what is happening, no consciousness that these are the final moments of his life, and therefore no worry or anxiety. From the dog's perspective it's just another injection – which he may not particularly enjoy – and, even if it causes him some momentary distress, that's not the same as being aware of what is happening and being distressed as a result.

I'll discuss the process of euthanasia shortly, as I think it's important that all dog owners are aware of what happens in order to be able to prepare themselves for the event, even if it is many years in the future. As I've said, the real mental anguish of euthanasia has to be borne not by the dog but by the owner, and understanding the process in advance can be a real help in coming to terms with what is going on when the day comes.

Before we get on to this final subject, it's worth discussing the crucial issue of timing – how do we know when the time has come to say goodbye to our beloved dog?

This is one of the most difficult subjects to tackle, and unfortunately there are no easy answers. Every dog, every owner and every vet is an individual with their own circumstances, views and feelings, and the combination of all these personal factors need to be taken into account in each case. What might be the right time for one dog may not be right for another, and it really is important to take the time to think this final decision through very carefully with input from all concerned – including, of course, the dog himself.

It's all too easy to forget the views of the animal at the centre of this decision in all the talk of quality of life, treatment options and prognosis.

It goes without saying that dogs can't tell us directly how they're feeling and if they are ready to go, but at this stage of life your relationship with your dog should be strong and deep enough to enable you to understand what your dog is trying subconsciously to tell you. I'm not talking about mystical supernatural powers here, just simple clues in his body language and behaviour that can help you understand how he is feeling and whether or not this is the right time to consider the end. For example, the fact that a dog who has always been fastidiously clean about the house starts to urinate indoors may indicate that he's gone beyond the point of caring about his world and life. Such clues need to be taken on board and used as evidence in the decision-making process if you are to get the timing right.

As mentioned, all dogs and situations are unique, but there are three key factors that I think usually give you a good idea about the state of your dog's quality of life in relation to the timing of euthanasia. The first is their desire to go for a walk. Some dogs are not keen walkers, in which case this factor is of less relevance, but for most dogs losing the desire to get up and out, even if it's only for a stroll around the patio, is one of the warning signs that the end may be near. Of course, there are lots of less serious reasons why a dog may go off their walks, such as lameness or simply inclement weather, but I'm talking here not about this factor in isolation, but as one sign taken in context of the dog's overall health situation and history.

Second is their appetite. Again, there are many factors that can influence appetite, the vast majority of which are not indicative of the end of life approaching – but a gradual decline in appetite which ultimately results in complete or almost complete inappetence can be another clear warning signal that the body is in terminal decline.

Finally, probably the most important factor of all is their relationship with you. In the final stages of life, the mind often deteriorates alongside the body and consciousness can be altered to such a degree that even loved ones are no longer recognised or reacted to. If this state is reached, with no clear underlying cause that your vet can identify, then it is likely to be a strong indicator that your dog has reached his final days.

By taking these three main issues into consideration, along with the other more individual clues from your dog, and talking to your family and veterinary surgeon, you will hopefully be able to come to the right decision. If in doubt at any point, it's better to err on the side of caution and give your dog a little longer, even if it's only a day or two. Eventually, however, it is nearly always kindest to have the courage to make a positive decision rather than waiting for nature to take its course. You need to be strong and brave for your dog's sake. Keeping a dog going for too long is an easy mistake to make and is something that many dog owners regret afterwards. Forcing yourself to think solely about your dog's welfare rather than your own feelings is incredibly hard, but it's vital that you make this final decision for your dog, not yourself.

Modern treatment options have introduced dilemmas to these final decisions. Years ago things were often simpler – a dog with cancer, or another serious disease, usually had little hope of survival and euthanasia was carried out as soon as palliative treatment failed to control the symptoms. Nowadays, the advent of so many new treatment options has made the decision-making process much harder and, in many cases, created an ethical minefield that can be very hard to navigate through.

The development of treatments such as advanced chemotherapy and radiotherapy for cancer, radical surgical options for tumours of the face and jaw and many more have made it much harder to say with any confidence that there is no chance of survival at any given point. While there can be no doubt that some of these new treatments offer remarkable results for small numbers of patients, in many more cases the practical reality of putting a dog through advanced treatments for serious diseases such as cancer can be far from a positive experience for them. Talk to some of the new breed of vets who are pioneering these therapies, and they will freely admit that in many cases the extra survival time that the new drugs or operations give can be measured in weeks rather than months or years, and much of that time is spent enduring side-effects from the treatment. With this in mind, I would question the place of some of these treatment options in compassionate veterinary medicine. In my view, too often these treatments are driven not by a simple desire to do what is best for the dog, but by a combination of technical and professional ambition on the part of the vet, and self-centred thinking on the part of the owner. It can be very hard to turn down a pioneering new treatment that offers the hope of a few more months with your beloved dog, especially if the costs are underwritten by a pet insurer, but I think there are many instances when the right thing to do is to say no and accept that the best thing for your dog is to allow the end to come as naturally as possible.

I am fully supportive of any treatment option that can extend a dog's life without having a negative impact on their quality of life, but I think we as a profession owe it to our patients and clients to be honest and always make treatment decisions with the best interests of the dog at heart rather than those of the owner or even vet.

Finally, it's time to consider the process of euthanasia itself. I'd like to emphasise that this shouldn't necessarily be viewed as a terrible, negative event. Instead, think of it as the final kindness that you are able to bestow on your dog, a release from his suffering that helps him slip away without the enduring pain of a natural end. It's not easy to think of the passing of a companion who may have been part of the family for 15 years or more in these terms, but it's important to focus on the positive aspects of what is about to happen. It is also important to allow yourself the opportunity to grieve once the deed is done. For your dog's sake, it is worth trying to stay composed and outwardly happy right up to the end as dogs are experts at picking up on human emotion.

The act of euthanasia is really very simple, and involves nothing more than a quick intravenous injection. The drug used is pentobarbitone, a powerful barbiturate that renders the dog unconscious within seconds of administration and stops the heart soon afterwards. I have given this injection to hundreds of dogs over the years and I still never cease to be amazed by the speed of its action and the peaceful end it brings. One hears tales of human executions where the unfortunate prisoner takes many minutes to die after a lethal injection, but, in my experience with dogs, the process is usually quick and painless with the dog often being unconscious before the injection is complete.

Once the injection has been administered and the vet has confirmed that your dog is dead, it's the right time to let all your emotion out and say a proper goodbye. Your vet will give you the space and time you need. Never, ever feel embarrassed about shedding tears in a vet's surgery – it is a normal and proper way to feel after such an emotional event and no vet worth his salt is going to take issue with your expressing your feelings however you need to.

Afterwards there is usually a decision to be made regarding the body, which you can either take home for burial if you have a suitable garden, or leave for the vet to arrange cremation, which is the usual option. As well as a routine cremation with other dogs, most vets also offer the option of an individual cremation where you can have your dog's ashes returned to you in a casket or urn. While this is usually a relatively expensive option, it does offer great comfort to many pet owners to feel that they have some physical essence of their dog to help them through the grieving process.

I hope this final chapter hasn't been a too depressing read, and it seems a sad note on which to end my book. But, as I've said, I don't personally see euthanasia as necessarily a sad event. It can represent a wonderful opportunity to release your dog from pain and suffering, and, if done properly, can be a fitting end to a loving relationship.

And, finally, there is one simple message I'd like to emphasise. Always remember that your relationship with your dog is like any other relationship, it needs a lifetime of love, care and attention to keep it healthy. Keep that in mind, and you won't go too far wrong.